Minder

annual 1986

CW01678014

£3.25

Contents

Annuals contents © by World International Publishing Limited.
All rights reserved throughout the world.

Published in Great Britain by
World International Publishing Limited.
P.O. Box 111, Gt. Ducie Street, Manchester M60 3BL.
Printed in Italy
SBN 7235 6750 6

Minder © Euston Films and Leon Griffiths.
Thames Television Limited, 148, Tottenham Court Road, London W1
Published under licence.

The Grilling of Shyster George

"Kindred spirits on the frontiers of free enterprise, Dave, gathered together to salute a fallen friend. On the slate, please," said Arthur in answer to Dave's question as to how Ozzie Duckworth's funeral had gone off earlier that morning. The expansiveness of Arthur's mood was down to the two large vodka and slims he had consumed at Maudi Duckworth's afterwards — that and the thought of the quick few folding ones he could make if Kenny Kirwan took the pizza toasters off his hands for the deckchairs he seemed so keen to unload. Back at Maudie's, Arthur had heard Monty Marshall mention he'd got an in with a roadside garden suppliers out at the spot near Epsom where he, Ozzie, and Binky Robertson had once all been arrested together. With a few poker burns on the deckchair frames to cover up the Clacton Council markings, he could easily bump them on to Monty as individually decorated sun recliners.

"Yes, Arthur, very noble," said Dave impatiently as he hooked Arthur another vodka from the optic and fished Terry's glass from under the tap. "But how's Maudie taking things?"

"Maudie's all right, Dave," said Terry affectionately, loosening his black tie. "The old girl's seen a bit in her time living with Ozzie. She's sweet as a pickle and tough as an old boot."

"Neither subtle nor tactful, but spoken truly, Terence," said Arthur, raising his glass to the widowed Maudie. "Let's hope she can keep Horizontal Bob and Billy the Bone under control now Ozzie's gone. The waters around those two have always been a little turbulent for the honest trader."

Ozzie Duckworth had always described himself, whenever social or legal convention dictated that he must, as a dealer in semi-precious metals. The semi-precious metals that he collected, separated, stacked, sorted and crushed came, for the most part, from MOT failures and the innards of gutted buildings, and they had proved semi-precious enough to buy him a large, detached family house close to the river, a small family fleet of regularly exchanged German cars, a villa on the Algarve, and a private education for his two sons. The physically rigorous disciplines of this education, with its emphasis on long runs, rugby and cold showers, had succeeded in turning them both into robust but vacuous nitwits, whilst leaving untapped any of the cannier qualities they might have inherited from their father. Regretfully having to recognise this fact when a heart attack forced him to retire, Ozzie had felt it wiser to let his sons continue their regular round of restaurants, racecourses and public houses, whilst handing the reins of his scrap metal business to George Chalmers, an accountant whose arithmetical dexterity, eye for a loophole and general deviousness had managed to give the company the appearance of running at a small but bearable loss in all but one of its thirty years of trading.

These skills of Georgie Chalmers, whose name, unwavering gaze and soft spoken manner of speech had conspired to land him with the nickname of 'Snaky', were considered of great public value by a large number of South Fulham's entrepreneurs, and consequently when, three weeks after Ozzie Duckworth's funeral, Snakey had telephoned Arthur from his home and asked for a meet at his office to discuss a little bit of business, Arthur had taken a taxi and told Terry to take the Jag round from the lock-up to the wholesale kitchen suppliers on Coronation Road and pick up the new crockery that 'Er Indoors was so keen to show off to her bridge circle.

It was from the kitchen centre he'd got the iffy toasters he'd managed to bump on to Kenny Kirwan for the deckchairs, and having shot the deckchairs through to Monty Marshall for three gross of haftless hoe blades, he'd got a friend of Terry's to wrap twine around the top half of the blades and bumped them back to the kitchen centre as traditional Indonesian vegetable dicers in exchange for 'Er Indoors' new crockery. It had been a long struggle, he reflected as he climbed out of the taxi and fished through his wallet for the fare. He was still quibbling with the driver over his tip when a man on a dumper truck full of timber and broken bricks started shouting for them to get a move on. When Arthur turned to remonstrate the taxi left with his fiver.

Arthur walked up the stairs to the three second storey rooms which constituted Snakey's business premises — one being the office of his secretary, Eve, whilst the other two were piled high with papers, brown envelopes, and files of a fictitious intricacy only Snakey and Eve could fathom — but when he got there Eve told him that George wasn't in yet.

"His car broke down again on the way here, Arthur," explained Eve. "The one you sold him. It's over at Pikey Jarrett's garage in Acton being fixed now. He's going to have to wait there till four. I'll make you a cup of tea if you want to wait."

"Thank you, Eve," said Arthur, picking up his hat, pulling back the cuff of his coat and tapping at his watch with the hand that held his cigar. "But whilst the sun is still high the wheels of commerce must be kept turning. You don't have an inkling as to what he might want, do you, Eve?"

"Something to do with Terry, Arthur," said Eve, folding a letter into a large envelope, putting another piece of paper into the typewriter roller, then picking up the polythene bag which contained her knitting. "He never says much, but I think he's in trouble."

"Trouble?" Arthur asked tentatively, smelling a fee then beginning to bluster about his workload in an attempt to establish how much. "Serious trouble, Eve? Of the kind that might need an elbow in the eye?"

"It's something to do with Ozzie Duckworth's boys," said Eve. "Ever since Maudie went to the Algarve with the cellist — you know, Wendy Whatsername who's got the music school over

Phil the Bookie's — Irish Leon's sister, the bloke who owns the cattery near the flyover at Chiswick . . .? Anyway," said Eve, regathering the thread of her story, "the moment Maudie was gone her boys started bothering George. I think there's unpleasantness in the air and he thought that perhaps Terry could help sort it out."

"You need have no worry on that score, Eve," said Arthur. "Terry dislikes a bully almost as much as I do. I shall make it my personal responsibility to see he gets straight over here the moment Snakey gets on the trumpet."

Outside, Arthur was standing on the step wondering whether, once Terry got back to the lock-up, it would be wise to send him round to Snakey's without further consultation about the fee, when a figure stepped out from where the pavement entered a narrow corridor of corrugated iron beneath some scaffolding and pulled a black polythene rubbish bag over his head.

"'Ere, you can't do this," he protested from inside the bag as he felt someone pushing him into the streets and heard the screech of tyres as he stumbled. "This is a violation of my inalienable rights as a British pedestrian. I shall . . ."

His words were cut off as he felt a hand in the small of his back shove him forward and he felt himself fall into the seat well of a car. Moments later he felt feet walking over him as the man who had pushed him climbed into the back of the car. Then the door slammed shut against the soles of his feet and the car pulled away.

"Is that you, Mister Chisholm?" asked Arthur nervously. "Mr Rycott? Whoever you are, I can promise you that you'll be hearing more than a few words concerning litigation from my solicitors the moment you . . ."

After threats of legal action provoked no reaction Arthur tried, somewhat less convincingly, threats of violence. Then he tried wriggling. This was followed by wheedling, cajoling and logical entreaty, dispensation from the kidnap on health grounds, renewed indignation, both feigned and real, then begging and offers of money. It was all to no avail. The man with his foot on the back of Arthur's neck made no reply.

"You're not going to enjoy what happens to you next," Arthur heard a voice say when, his avenues of persuasion seemingly exhausted, he had lapsed into silence. He heard the man in the front of the car begin to giggle, a thin half aspirated sound devoid of warmth, and he swallowed. He found himself counting every bump that the car went over. Each one seemed more ominous than the last. Then suddenly the car stopped, the door opened and he felt hands manhandling him to his feet. From out of the bottom of the bag he could see his shoes and the black, hard packed earth beneath them.

"All right then, lock him in the storage box with Little Sheba until he comes through with what he's done with the money," said a voice, and Arthur realised suddenly and fearfully that he was in Ozzie Duckworth's scrap yard.

"You're making a mistake . . ." he started, but the words were choked off in a wail of alarm as he felt someone grab hold of his arm and rush him across the open ground to where the storage box and Little Sheba were waiting.

The storage box, Arthur remembered, was an old thirty-foot

container set up on railway sleepers where various engines and transmission parts for freshly broken trucks were kept, whilst Little Sheba was a ferociously bad tempered Alsatian that Ozzie had let roam loose at night as a guard dog. Once, when Arthur had been round the yard on a spot of urgent about some pinball machines, Little Sheba had flown out at him from underneath a Range Rover snarling like something out of a video nasty. Even today, Arthur often found himself wondering what accident of fate could have caused Little Sheba to become entangled in her chain with her jaws clattering like castanets an inch or so from his kneecaps.

"This is a case of wrongful kidnap, mistaken identity and all that," he protested as he felt himself shoved into the storage box, heard a dog snarl, and then heard the container door slam behind him. He knew, even with a black polythene bag over his head, that he was in pitch darkness.

There was silence for a moment, then a low, querulous growling sound that snapped suddenly into a snarl. "Oh, my good God," Arthur mumbled through rustling polythene as he struggled to free himself from the bag.

There was silence again, then a soft scuttering sound of paws and claws crossing the metal floor towards him. The sound ceased somewhere in the darkness in front of him and Arthur, his senses honed sharp by fear, felt Little Sheba's eyes pierce the darkness as it measured its leap.

"Nice doggie," whimpered Arthur in the darkness. "Roll over. Play dead."

There was a sudden crack as a bolt went back, loud as a gunshot, and Arthur hunched up his shoulders and put his hands up over his face. When he brought them down again the container door had been thrown open, and standing in front of him, growling once again, was Jess, a small Jack Russell bitch that Ozzie Duckworth kept in the caravan at the yard to keep down the rat population. At the far end of the box, curled up on an old coat in front of a stack of gearboxes, was a recent litter of pups.

"All right, George," said a voice behind him. "Next time it's not pretend. Either you tell us what you've done with the old man's dough or we get Little . . ."

The voice trailed off into surprised silence as Arthur turned round. Looking up at him were Horizontal Bob and Billy the Bone. Standing on either side of them holding open the doors of the container were two tall, pale-skinned men wearing long leather coats and, despite the blustery October weather, sporting sunshades.

"Idiot!" Billy the Bone said to them angrily. "This isn't Chalmers. This is Arthur Daley."

"That's what I was trying to tell

you before you threw me in there with that savage beast," said Arthur indignantly as he brushed down his overcoat and climbed awkwardly down from the container. "What's the matter with you two lads? Have all those shampoo bubbles so softened up your grey matter that you think nothing of abducting a citizen about his lawful business and then, under very great duress and discomfort, I might add . . ."

"Shut up, Arthur," said Horizontal Bob, putting a hand on his shoulder in a manner that managed to be both friendly and menacing. Arthur, his hand halfway to his jacket pocket for the reassurance of a fresh cigar, decided to keep quiet. "Just because we made a mistake doesn't mean that we're stupid, Arthur," said Horizontal Bob.

"You should understand that," said Billy the Bone. "Georgie Chalmers is a smart alec. A clever dick. A jumped up little office boy who tried to steal from the old man. He's a louse, a liar and a thief. Is it our fault you bear such a strong resemblance to him? Just because you're not George Chalmers doesn't mean that you don't know where he is."

"I wish I could help you there, Billy," said Arthur cheerfully, and with some obvious relief, "but I haven't seen Snakey for quite some time now. Haven't heard from him, either."

"Don't lie, Arthur," said Billy the Bone. "You were picked up on his doorstep. You know where he is."

"Billy, on my life as a loyal friend of your father's — God rest his soul — I swear to you that I have no idea where to find Snakey Chalmers. If I could help you, I would. Believe me."

"Bob," said Billy the Bone absently, as if he had only been half listening to Arthur's words. "Go and get Sheba. Arthur — you get back in the box."

The trouble with Arthur, thought Terry as he drove the Jag down the Goldhawk Road toward the corner where Arthur had said he would meet him, was that whilst most people were either one step ahead of the game, or one step behind it, Arthur was still worrying whether he'd turned out in the right shirt. Who else but Arthur would phone the lock-up and tell him to drop whatever it was that he was doing when all he'd been doing anyway for the last two hours was wait for Arthur?

Terry pulled over at the side of the road beside the long corrugated iron fence which marked the boundary of Ozzie Duckworth's scrapyard, and looked around for Arthur. Presently he saw Arthur peer out from behind a thick trunked tree that stood at the edge of the pavement. He glanced up and down the street then hurried across to the car and leaned in through the window. "Terry, you're going to have to be quick now. They've got Snakey in there and they want blood."

"Hold on, now," said Terry, trying to calm him. "Who's after whose blood?"

"Horizontal Bob and Billy the Bone are after dismantling Snakey Chalmers. They've pulled one of their strokes and sent a snatch squad after the poor geezer. Right now they've probably got him locked up with Little Sheba. I want you to go in there now, Terry, and sort those two out. They're a menace to honest traders. And if Snakey happens to mention a fee to you, just refer him to me."

"Arthur, how many of them are there in there?"

"Four. Not counting Snakey. You should be able to handle them. I'll stay out here and . . ."

"No you won't, Arthur. Get in," said Terry. Arthur swallowed nervously but did as he was told. "And while we're about it," said Terry as he climbed into the passenger seat, "how come you know all this?"

"Know all what?" asked Arthur innocently.

"All about what's happening to Snakey in there, Arthur," said Terry, pulling away from the kerb.

"Because I was in there myself until an hour ago. I still would be if I hadn't . . . or rather, if they hadn't got hold of Snakey," said Arthur, putting a gloved hand to the dash as Terry swung the Jag through the open gates of the yard.

Terry drove around a pile of junked fridges and rusty girders, along past the caravan that served as a yard office, and towards the storage container at the far side of the yard. As they approached they saw Georgie Chalmers backed up against one of the side walls with Billy the Bone holding Little Sheba on a short chain in front of him. Little Sheba was yapping excitedly at him. The two geezers in the sunglasses blocked any thought of flight to either side that Georgie might have harboured, whilst Horizontal Bob stood behind his brother tapping his toe with the tip of a crowbar that dangled from his hand.

Terry put his foot down and drove straight at them. He was

five yards from them when, as he'd expected, they scattered.

Little Sheba broke free from Billy the Bone's grip and set off after the two men in sunglasses who scrambled up across a heap of old tyres, kicking at the Alsatian as they went.

Terry stepped out of the car and ducked under Horizontal Bob's wild swing with the crowbar. He struck him a sharp one on his nose and Bob went down, as horizontal as he'd ever been. Terry felt Billy the Bone's arms around his neck and ducked forward, rolling him over his shoulder. As he did so he saw Snakey Chalmers making a dash for the car and heard its engines start. Billy half scrambled to his feet and then the sole of Terry's shoe sent him over again.

"Arthur!" yelled Terry, and leaving the two brothers, he set off after Arthur who was backing the Jag towards the yard's entrance. Terry caught up, opened the door, and climbed in.

"Thanks, Terry," said Georgie Chalmers. "Those boys are hopeless. The simplest matter of creative accounting seems beyond them. The money they're looking for is in a Portuguese bank account out in the Algarve with Maudie. She dishes them out so much every week to play with. Looking at those two I sometimes think Ozzie would have been better off just paying tax. If there's ever anything I can do for you, Terry."

"Nah, forget it, Snakey. It's partly Arthur's fault that you ended up in there in the first place."

"Terence," said Arthur indignantly as he turned to steer the Jag out through the yard gates, "are you suggesting that the fact that Billy and Bob picked Snakey up at Pikey Jarrett's garage is down to me?"

"Yes, Arthur," said Terry disgustedly, "that's exactly what I'm suggesting."

"Terence. Snakey. For three hours I was locked in the back of that box with a beast whose primal instincts are to maim and kill, but I spoke not a word, Snakey, not a word." He turned to face Snakey as he spoke and the mask of sincerity on his face crumpled into an expression of abject fear. Peering through the window with its paws on the sill was Little Sheba. Arthur pressed down on the accelerator in panic and the Jag shot out backwards across the road and into a skip that stood on its far side. There was the sound of breaking crockery in the boot.

Passing through the lock~up

Terry has helped Arthur load and unload all the articles listed below at one time or another. By reading up, down, forwards, backwards or diagonally, can you spot the following articles?

APRONS
BALLOONS
BELTS
CARDS
CASH REGISTERS
COMBS
COMPUTERS
CRAYONS
CUDDLY TOYS
GOLD BALLS
HULA HOOPS
LAMPS
LEATHER JACKETS
PARTY HATS
PERFUMES
RADIOS
SHOES
SOAP
SOCKS
STRING
TENTS
TOASTERS
TOY SOLDIERS
TRINKETS
TROPICAL FISH
TROUSERS
TYPEWRITERS
VIDEO TAPES
WHISTLES
WIGS

S	B	M	O	C	P	S	R	E	I	D	L	O	S	Y	O	T	X	O
W	E	B	L	D	S	T	E	K	C	A	J	R	E	H	T	A	E	L
H	Y	P	A	D	O	L	N	T	S	Y	O	U	T	C	D	G	F	A
S	L	X	A	L	J	E	T	P	E	R	F	U	M	E	S	Y	X	B
P	O	V	N	T	L	B	O	T	U	B	O	T	S	E	O	H	S	K
F	W	I	G	S	O	O	N	L	I	S	R	R	E	S	E	D	T	I
L	S	Z	D	Y	H	E	O	T	X	O	E	W	F	O	N	Z	W	P
G	I	F	E	A	I	L	D	N	P	T	U	O	T	A	M	O	A	P
N	O	S	L	S	R	E	P	I	S	R	E	T	U	P	M	O	C	L
I	B	U	O	C	A	L	C	I	V	E	R	C	X	D	G	M	R	E
R	H	C	S	W	H	A	G	F	I	S	T	A	H	Y	T	R	A	P
T	K	N	M	D	L	E	K	J	C	U	D	D	L	Y	T	O	Y	S
S	O	A	P	F	R	Q	S	T	U	S	L	L	A	B	F	L	O	G
W	X	A	I	H	P	A	P	R	O	N	S	C	O	L	L	Y	N	A
G	E	S	S	Y	O	U	C	R	G	O	L	P	F	I	S	K	S	P
P	H	A	O	T	Y	P	E	W	R	I	T	E	R	S	Z	N	P	O
H	C	S	T	N	E	T	A	M	B	O	U	R	I	B	B	O	M	S
S	R	E	S	U	O	R	T	R	I	N	K	E	T	S	G	L	A	X
T	R	A	S	E	L	T	S	I	H	W	Z	A	B	N	A	H	L	O

Brief Encounter II

Izzy Nibbs looked up from the drawing board in his sixth floor office and offered Arthur his ink-stained hand. Arthur touched it briefly and took a seat.

"Izzy Nibbs," said Izzy. "I got the Nibbs bit at school — I was always drawing, you see. Iz came later and then Izzy. It seems to have stuck."

"Very interesting." Arthur was relieved he hadn't bothered lugging the copier up with him. It was heavy, it leaked, and it didn't look as if Izzy could afford it. "Hughie said you might be in some bother."

For a second, Izzy's eyes looked puzzled behind the bottle lenses. "It's all the drawing," he explained. "Tires the peepers. I'd never have thought about going to an optician. Not until that time I fell in the soup when I was trying to read that sailor's tattoo."

Arthur thought better of mentioning the artwork he needed for his musical Christmas card venture.

"Do I understand you are looking for some kind of retribution?" he asked, matter-of-factly.

"No, no," insisted Izzy. "That's all over with now. The thing is, I had no idea I needed spectacles. I thought everybody saw things the way I did." Izzy took off his glasses and squinted round his dingy office. "Even when I walked through that plate glass window I thought it was a bit of bad luck."

"You're beginning to lose me here, Izzy. I'm a businessman, not a mince pie mechanic."

Izzy got up and walked to the window. He pulled the lace curtain a few inches to one side and beckoned Arthur to join him. Below them, on the other side of the street, a man stood in front of a tobacconist's in the pouring rain. He was well over six feet tall and nearly as broad. Long strands of wet hair were whipped across his face by the fierce wind. His rumpled, dripping coat flapped around his knees. When he slowly raised his head and gazed up at the window, Arthur felt an unpleasant tingling at the base of his spine. "They call him Crusher," whispered Izzy, shuddering involuntarily as he let the curtain fall back. "Nobody can pronounce his real name. He comes from Armenia. They say he killed three men in a fight over a goose."

Arthur took a deep breath through pursed lips.

Izzy sat down. "It was my testimony that got him put away," he continued. "I heard the alarm at the supermarket going off and then this huge shape sprinted past me. I was sure it was him — but that was before I knew I needed glasses."

"And now you think he's out to get revenge?"

Izzy nodded wistfully. "It wouldn't have been so bad if he'd gone quietly. Knocked four coppers out before they got him handcuffed to a drainpipe. Then he pulled that from the wall and set about the van with it. I think they finally brought him down with a tranquiliser gun." Izzy distractedly inked in the ears of the rabbit he was drawing. "After that he took a warder hostage on the roof of the jail and demanded two million in gold and a seat on the space shuttle. He was up there six days before he settled for twenty double cheeseburgers and two gallons of orangeade."

Arthur lifted his eyebrows and thoughtfully watched the ash from his cigar fall to the floor. "Dealing with your demented forefinger can be very expensive," he offered. "Very expensive indeed."

Izzy's face fell. "You don't think I should try and pay him off instead?" he asked.

Arthur reared suddenly forward in his chair, shaking his head and waving his cigar hand so fast it was almost a blurr. "Don't misunderstand me, Izzy. I'm sure we can come to some arrangement. In fact, I think I know just the man for the job. Here's my card. I'll be in touch later."

Arthur let himself out of Izzy's office building and was opening the front door of a left-hand drive Merc when Detective Sergeant Rycott pulled up in front of him. Arthur noticed that Crusher had taken this as a signal to make himself scarce.

"Daley," sneered Rycott, climbing out of his car. "Don't tell me you're the revenge crazed killer

that's put an almighty wind up Mr Nibbs? That even now, you're fleeing hotfoot from the wrath of the long arm of the law?"

Arthur climbed into his car and shut the door.

Rycott tapped on the window and Arthur wound it down. "As far as I'm concerned, Mr Rycott, the long arm of the law hasn't got a leg to stand on. We can't all look to the mother state for our bread and butter. I was seeing my old friend Izzy on business. I'm thinking of expanding." He ignored Rycott's pointed glance at his waistline. "I wanted to discuss the logo for my new project. Something to put on the door. Something tasteful, informative. Gold leaf on leather perhaps — something to suit my status."

"Your status would be better represented in chalk on hardboard — with a damp sponge hanging nearby. Where's your tax disc?"

"Take a look at the front. These are trade plates. I'm on my way to pick up an MOT."

"Very good, Arthur. What's in the back?"

"Is it true," asked Arthur, irritably opening the boot, "that when all the snakes were chased out of Ireland, they swam over here and joined the police force?"

"I'd hate to have your nerve in a tooth," said Rycott, looking uninterestedly into a cardboard box full of ceramic models of a mongoose fighting a cobra. "Wildlife of England?" read Rycott, dropping the model back in the box. "You'd better take hold of yourself, Daley — I think you're running out of string."

Arthur called in at *the Winch* for Terry, and when they'd picked up the MOT certificate they made their way to Hughie Miles' fancy goods shop.

Hughie greeted them warmly and helped them unload the boxes of ceramic wildlife into the back room. It was only when Hughie brought out a large jar and three new glasses they realised exactly how far out of character he was behaving. "Cherries in brandy," he said gleefully, spooning some into the glasses. "And none of your common muck, either. My auntie's French. She buys them from the supermarket. I trust an extra large one is in order?" There was a dreadful smile on his face as he held a dark cherry to his lips. Arthur looked at Terry. Terry shrugged. "I mean," Hughie went on, eating the flesh of the cherry and flicking the stone into a large metal ashtray, "I can assume that everything's been satisfactorily concluded, can't I?"

"You can rest easy about those animals," said Arthur, recounting Hughie's money. "They are absolutely first class. They've been laminated. And as for the jam jar, there's nothing on the clock but the maker's name."

"Not the models, Arthur," laughed Hughie. "Or the car. You know . . . that other business."

"That other business?" repeated Arthur, trying not to meet Hughie's manic gaze. He bit into a cherry and tried to drop the stone into the ashtray. It stuck to his finger.

"Yes, you know . . . Crusher. I take it Terry sent him packing with a flea in his ear? I hope you didn't have to break anything, Terry."

Arthur squeezed the stone between thumb and forefinger. It shot across the room and bounced off a glass case containing a stuffed owl. The cat on top of the case briefly opened his yellow eyes.

"What you on about?" asked Terry, leaving his cherries alone and sipping his brandy.

"Crusher. You did get rid of him, didn't you, Terry?" Hughie was beginning to shake.

Arthur swallowed another cherry and flicked the stone off his finger with his thumb. It stuck to his thumb. Arthur flicked his hand and the stone fell to the carpet. He tried to push it under his chair with his foot.

"It's a nice little job I've got for you," Arthur explained, wiping his hand on the side of the chair Hughie couldn't see. "A bit of the short, sharp, shock treatment."

"You mean he's still on the loose?" gulped Hughie.

Arthur frowned at him. "It's all under control, Hughie. Though I can't see why you're concerned."

Hughie's behaviour suddenly slipped back into its more usual, hysterically put upon groove. "Of course I'm concerned, you toerag. If Crusher gets past Izzy, he'll be after me!" Hughie took his handkerchief from his pocket and began wiping his hands.

"I don't understand any of this," said Terry, sipping his drink.

Hughie paced up and down the room like a caged rat. "I helped finger him, you twerps! I was driving past the supermarket when a police car blocked the road. I got out and told them which way he'd gone."

"You did what?" asked Arthur. Hughie's return to normality was making his teeth ache.

"I didn't know which way, did I? I just pointed and said 'go get 'im.' I didn't know they'd catch anyone. I just didn't want them searching my car. I'm not standing still while plod pulls me with a boot full of your mini computers."

Arthur spluttered with rage. "Those computers were the real thing. The line was discontinued and they wanted the warehouse space. All you needed was an adaptor and an Arabic dictionary and —"

"I wasn't to know they were kosher, was I, Arthur? And then when this fellow Nibbs backed up my story — I had to go through with it. I had no choice."

"You're not telling me you grassed an innocent man?" asked Arthur, a note of stern disapproval creeping into his voice.

Hughie sat down and slapped his forehead. "I didn't know he

was innocent. I didn't know anything. He already had form."

"Once a man's debt to society has been paid," began Arthur, "no man has the right to . . . Hughie? Hughie — what's the matter?"

Hughie kept silent as his shaking dramatically increased. He walked to the door and stared into the shop. Arthur followed his gaze through the front window. Striding purposefully down the street towards them, his wild wet hair flying in the wind and rain, his teeth bared in a hideous grin, his face flushed with greedy anticipation, was the massive bulk of Crusher.

"It's him!" gasped Hughie, pushing them into the shop. "Help me!" He slammed the door shut and locked it from the inside.

"This is the 'little job'?" asked Terry sarcastically.

When Crusher walked in, Terry picked up a small box of pencils and handed Arthur ten pence.

"That won't be all, will it, sir?" Arthur begged. Terry pretended to be examining some india rubbers shaped like famous pop stars as Crusher's huge bulk loomed over Arthur.

"Yes?" whispered Arthur.

Crusher's head swivelled slowly round the room. Arthur imagined he could see the carbuncle on his neck pulsating. Crusher rapped his sausage-like fingers on a tray of Zirconian jewellery. A small puddle formed on the glass. "I want them all," he said softly.

Arthur picked up the whole tray and pushed it at him.

"How much?" asked Crusher.

Arthur did some quick calculations in his head. "To you, sir — £200."

Crusher took out his wallet. Arthur could see it was empty except for some credit cards. He pulled a single cheque from his top pocket and began writing. Arthur restrained an impluse to cough. "A cheque will do?" asked Crusher, noting Arthur's uneasiness. Arthur nodded silently.

Crusher took the tray of jewellery, put down the cheque and walked out of the shop. It took two minutes of banging on the door before Hughie opened up. Arthur was explaining exactly what had happened when the phone rang. Arthur answered it. It was Izzy.

"Well, I had to pay him, didn't I?" the comic book illustrator reasoned. "He came round just after the police left. Asked if I needed any jobs doing . . ." The line fell silent for a few seconds as Izzy relived a particularly nasty memory. "I mean, I helped put him away, didn't I? And there's lots of legitimate jobs around an office that call for an axe and a power drill, aren't there? After all, it's Friday — I've got a deadline to meet and . . . well, I'm glad it's off my conscience at last."

"How much?" asked Arthur. Seconds later he turned to Hughie with a broad smile on his face as he put the phone down. "Looks like I got you a result, son."

"What do you mean?" asked Hughie.

"I mean 200 little green men is well below the market rate for buying off your drooling mass murderer." Arthur didn't hear the bell of the shop sounding behind him. "Your really vicious head squeezing slob won't be fobbed off with —"

"You!" Crusher's booming voice interrupted Arthur's spiel. He was standing in the doorway clutching the tray of jewellery. Beside him was Ramone Silver, a.k.a. Mouse McCartney, a one-time circus acrobat who now spent his time collecting half finished beer glasses in any pub that would let him in.

"Me?" asked Arthur, putting his finger to his chest.

Crusher nodded. "My friend here doesn't believe I just bought these. He says he won't pay me £25 for them."

"£25!" said Hughie angrily. "If that's all you wanted, why didn't you ask?"

Crusher stared at him with a puzzled frown. Mouse eyed the jewels greedily. "You say I didn't buy these?" he asked, turning to Arthur and bunching up his massive fist.

Terry stepped forward. "Hold on," he said quietly. "There's no need for — "

Hughie leapt on Crusher's back with a scream of hysterical anguish. Crusher reached back one hand and threw him into a pile of furry dinosaurs. Terry moved in with his guard high and Mouse jammed an empty cardboard box over his head and shoulders. Terry swung wildly and Crusher pushed him head first into a stack of dartboards. Terry pulled the box off his head and took guard again. Crusher smiled and waded in, swinging roundhouse rights and lefts. Terry let him come, then dropped to a crouch, burying a ferocious combination of hooks and jabs into his colossal belly. He ducked out of Crusher's attempted bear hug, dug an elbow hard into the small of the big man's back then put his full weight behind three clubbing blows to the ear. Crusher staggered through some baskets full of running shoes, knocked over a rack of day-glo t-shirts and steadied himself with one hand on a wobbly table inlaid with an underwater scene of a shark, an open chest of treasure and a shipwrecked galleon. He shook his head, smiled even broader and rushed at Terry.

Terry's hand closed round the nearest object. When he saw it was a rubber hammer he threw it to one side and tried to jab. His blows hit home but Crusher kept on coming. Terry swayed, dodging Crusher's wild blows, then unleashed four more hard hooks to the body with machine gun rapidity and followed them up with two hard right crosses that turned Crusher on his feet and sent him flopping against a shelf covered

with executive toys. Terry just had time to see Arthur crawling out of the door on his hands and knees before Mouse joined forces with Crusher and the battle began in earnest. Terry remembered the taste of blood in his mouth, a futuristic mobile that fell from the ceiling when he grabbed it for support, and the distant sound of a police siren. And then everything went cold and black.

The following Monday, back in the shop, neither Terry nor Arthur were getting much change from Hughie Miles.

"It's a matter of principle," said Arthur as Hughie tried to fix up a new shelf. "We stood by you in your hour of need."

"But I didn't need you, Arthur," Hughie replied. "The police took care of everything. I even got Terry off that charge of causing an affray."

"Thanks a million," scowled Terry, gently rubbing his teeth with his fingers.

Hughie put down his hammer. "Don't forget I had to drop the assault charges against Crusher too," he explained. "If it hadn't been for the fact that I'd got him bang to rights for passing me that dud cheque it could have been bad for you."

"You talk more like plod every day," said Arthur in disgust. "My man lays down his very life for you and —"

"Forget it, Arthur," said Terry, getting up to leave. "He's not worth it." As he turned to the door he saw Crusher walking in, a pained smile on his battered features.

"You should be in jail!" said Hughie, edging for the back door.

Crusher shook his head. "I did nothing wrong," he explained. "It was you who attacked me. These people saw it. And then you accused me of fraud. And then you had me locked away for a second time."

"Hold on," said Terry wearily as Crusher advanced on Hughie. "I don't feel up to another twelve rounder."

"There's no chance of that, Terry," Crusher continued. "You see, my cheque was cleared by the bank this morning and the police

dropped all charges. Of course my solicitor has advised me that I can expect handsome compensation over the matter of defamation, loss of earnings, assault and false arrest."

"And it was you who grassed the man in the first place," Arthur pointed out.

Hughie's resistance crumbled. "Will you settle out of court?" he asked feebly.

Ten minutes later, Crusher had pocketed a wad full of notes and Hughie was asking him to repeat his promise that he'd never bother him again. Crusher nodded slowly and gave him a look that Hughie could feel on the back of his skull. "You'll be all right now," he said. "But keep taking the careful pills."

Later, as Terry and Arthur drove Crusher back to his lodgings, Terry looked across the front seat at his battered opponent with grudging respect. "Are you really Armenian?" he asked.

Crusher shook his head. "That was part of my circus act. Mouse dreamed it up. Just like he dreamed up this little caper." He stopped riffling through the wad of notes and handed Terry four fifties. "You fight a good fight."

"You're no slouch yourself. Now, I'm not condoning what Izzy and Hughie did, but did you really have to —"

"It was pride, Terry," interrupted Crusher. "Sheer pride. Once I decided to go straight, I thought I owed it to myself to go out on a high note."

"You're going straight?"

"As a locomotive. But first I had to get back my self respect. And I couldn't have done it any other way. The supermarket's been pulled down."

"So?"

"So I wouldn't have minded one more crack at it. That night was the first time I'd tripped an alarm in seven years . . ."

There was a gurgle from the back seat. Arthur leaned forward. "You mean —?"

"It was a moment of weakness, Arthur," explained Crusher.

"Good job you weren't feeling strong," Arthur commented. "You'd have stolen the whole building!"

One of Our Boxes is MISSING

Terry had been in *The Winchester* since opening time. Last night at the lock-up, after they'd boxed off the last of the eight hundred *Teach Yourself Bulgarian Cookery* video cassettes and loaded them into the boot of Arthur's Jag, Arthur had said he'd be in *The Winch* with Terry's wages the following morning. Now, with time hurrying onwards, Arthur still hadn't shown and the question of whether or not Terry would be able to clear his lunchtime slate rested on a steward's enquiry at Ripon.

Between trips to the turf accountant and reading the paper Terry had been holding a much interrupted conversation with Dave — a conversation that had grown increasingly rambling as the time had worn on and the day had worn off. They had started on the relative abilities of Jesper Olsen and John Chedozie as measured against their respective transfer fees, had stopped off at the price of Danish bacon and the amounts of money in the modern game, then trodden a nostalgic path back, via the skills of Charlie Cooke, Jimmy Greaves and Johnny Haynes, to Dave's boyhood memories of Len Shackleton. From there the conversation had taken off for penguins and polar exploration, in particular whether it had been another bloke called Shackleton or Sir Walter Scott who had discovered the North Pole. Dave was just explaining to Terry that he was getting the bloke who discovered the North Pole confused with the geezer who'd invented cigarettes when Arthur came in. The expression on his face indicated, as it had done for the last month and a half, that all was not well. In fact this afternoon's expression suggested that all was worse than ever.

"Better make it a large one, Dave," Arthur advised gloomily. "Every son of toil deserves a brief moment's respite from that desperate race between death and the postdated cheque. Put it on Terry's slate, will you?"

"Glad you said that, Arthur," said Dave. "I've been meaning to bring up the question of your own slate. I know you've had a hard time of it, but it's been three months now."

"And before you go putting drinks on my slate how about giving me what I've got in the pipe? I been waiting here for four blinking hours."

"Dave! Terry! Please! Not now," said Arthur, sounding like an adult whose intricately laid plans were being threatened by unruly children. "You know I've had to batten hatches on the fruits of my labour. In the circumstances it's been the only safe thing to do."

"Down to his last fifty grand in readies, the recession's beginning to bite," said Terry sarcastically.

"You can leave out the cheap jibes, Terry," said Arthur, his face a mask of wounded trust, his hand raised in the air to halt such heartless levity. "Forget the bantering bonhommie. I've got a job for you. I've seen him, Terry."

"Seen who?"

"The black hole in my finances is who. That unprincipled little con artist from the colonies. The cause of my current ag, the wellspring of my woe. Docherty." He pronounced the name much as a doctor might pronounce the name of a particularly unpleasant virus. Terry and Dave's only response was a groan of impatience.

"Don't you ever stop?" asked Terry. "So you lost a couple of grand. Forget it. Forget Douglas Docherty. They're both over the hills and far away by now."

"No they're not, Terry. You think I'd forget a face that owes me? I saw him coming out of a shop down Holland Park."

"It's sad to see a man reduced to this, innit?" said Terry. "Clutching at straws. Seeing faces he recognises in the crowd. Thinks everyone's laughing at him."

"Reckon you're right, Tel," said Dave. "It'll be doctors in white coats next."

The last round of mockery proved too much for Arthur. He put his hat back on his head, his cigar between his teeth, and turned to leave. "If you don't want the job, Terry, simply say so. If you do, there's two hundred sovs to go with the fifty I already owe you. Just help me find him and my five grand."

"I thought you said you'd lost three grand," said Terry, climbing down from his bar stool, shrugging at Dave and following Arthur toward the door.

"Did I?" asked Arthur innocently as he held the door open for Terry.

"Yes, you did," said Terry as he walked through it.

"Well, I thought that if you were going to give him a good pasting to get back my three grand we might as well call it five," explained Arthur as Terry looked at him in disgust.

Douglas Docherty, the cause of Arthur's current ag, was a tall, softly spoken young Canadian from Toronto. He and Arthur had first met in a country pub, *The Black Bull*, where Arthur and Binky Robertson had been forced to take refuge when Arthur's car had broken down on the way back from a day at Newmarket races. Arthur had phoned *The Winch* to tell Terry that they were

stuck — alone, friendless, and far from home — while Binky went to order the drinks from the cocktail lounge. However, when Dave had reminded Arthur that he'd sent Terry up west with 'Er Indoors' nephew to see he didn't get into too much trouble on his stag night, Arthur had realised he was going to have to stay there for the evening. Binky, who had spent almost as much money in the racecourse bar as he had at the Tote window, was soon in bed, and Arthur, eager to recoup some of the five pounds he had lost in an ill-advised plunge on one of Binky's tips, had tried to interest the hotel's landlord in some nice pieces of Jacobean oak which would add immeasurably to the rural charm of his establishment. The landlord, used to the ways of city folk stopping overnight on their way to or from the races, had told him, fairly politely, to get knotted.

It was then that Douglas Docherty, who had overheard their conversation, introduced himself to Arthur. He said he was over in this country buying antiques for sale back in Canada and that, to save him making costly and time-consuming trips to and fro across the Atlantic, he was looking for someone with enough knowledge of the antique trade to work the English half of the operation. By half past two in the morning, Arthur had had an in. Douglas would deliver a container to the lock-up; Arthur, through his contacts, would buy Victorian furniture, and pack it and send it to Toronto. Douglas would meet the container there, unpack it, then sell it, either direct to shops, or at open auction.

For a few months things had gone well. So well that Terry, tired of spending his days in a dark container trying to squeeze pianos, dressers and bedding boxes into spaces where they wouldn't go, had asked for a rise. Faced with this, Arthur had moved the operation to a disused bobbin factory behind his car lot and employed a gormless young man called Midge to do the same thing for next to nothing under his version of the Youth Training Scheme. Arthur, although convinced that this particular youth could not be trained in any task more complicated than changing the cassette on his Walkman, which he wore all day at work, had been pleased to do his bit to help the government in its tooth and nail fight against unemployment, and for a while longer the enterprise had continued to flourish.

Then two months before, disaster had struck. There had been no cheque from Douglas, and Arthur, despite repeated phone calls to the two Toronto numbers that Douglas had left, had been unable to contact him. Meanwhile, enquiries to the container company had revealed that the last box of furniture had been shipped not to Toronto but Miami, where it had been collected by a Mister Smith. On receipt of this information Arthur had let Midge and the bobbin factory go and sworn that never again would he go racing with Binky Robertson.

"Binky's unreliable, Terry," explained Arthur as they drove toward Holland Park. "A real friend would have stood by me and stopped me getting involved. Just like I stood by him at the race-course, trying to stop him doing anything silly with his money."

"Arthur, you went there to try and flog him that Daimler you'd bought from the funeral company," Terry reminded him as Arthur pulled up at the antique shop where he thought he'd seen Douglas Docherty.

"Fat lot of good it did me, too," said Arthur, climbing out of the car. "The money for that went up the Swannee on a horse that an old school friend of Binky's said was a sure thing in the three o'clock. I'm still counting the damage from that one myself."

In the antique shop a young man with long hair tied back in a pony tail, an earring in his left ear and a purple silk neckerchief tied with studied casualness above the open neck of a collarless shirt, eyed them both with distaste before asking what they wanted. Arthur, attempting to appear casual, asked the price of a pair of matching Regency spitoons, winced at the man's reply, then asked him if he'd seen a shifty little colonial git who looked like the type who'd steal pennies off dead men's eyes.

The man looked blank and Terry explained that they were looking for a Canadian by the name of Douglas Docherty.

After a moment's thought the man told them that there'd been a Canadian in there that morning looking for Victorian and Edwardian furniture and that he had sent him to Bernard, a friend and fellow dealer who had a shop down the Islington end of Camden Passage and who dealt in the kind of stuff that the Canadian had been looking for.

"You see what he was asking for them spitters, Terry?" Arthur asked when they were back in the car and headed for Camden Passage. "The man's got more front than Southend. Wisest thing I ever did, getting out of the antique game. Nowadays it's full of robbers who aren't prepared to let the other man make an honest sov."

"Then you should have felt right at home there, Arthur. Anyway, you got out of it because you were conned," Terry pointed out.

"If you choose to see my financial misfortune in those terms I'll thank you to keep quiet about it, Terence," said Arthur. "After all, I've my reputation as a businessman to consider."

"It'll cost you," said Terry with a chuckle.

"Terence, I never thought I'd hear you stoop to such tactics," said Arthur. "I'm deeply shocked. How much?"

"Just the fifty you owe me. After all, what are mates for?"

At Camden Passage they found that Bernard wasn't in. However, a bored looking brunette reading the *Telegraph* told them that Douglas Docherty had been in about an hour earlier. Arthur asked her if she knew where Douglas had gone and Terry asked her what she was doing that evening. She gave Arthur the name of the hotel where Douglas was staying and told Terry that she was going to the theatre with her boyfriend who was a black belt in karate. Terry said that he'd done some

Jag again and he began to mimic Midge. " 'Finking of starting up on my own.' That boy couldn't start a car on his own. The problem with kids like him is too much money and no sense of discipline. He probably needs written instructions on how to shave in the mornings. Even then they'd have to be simple with plenty of pictures. Reminds me of what old Tony Iggledon used to say . . ." But Terry had stopped listening and was concentrating on the evening traffic.

The receptionist at the hotel told them that Douglas Docherty was in room seventy on the third floor. In the lift on the way up there, Arthur explained to Terry how he wanted him to kick open the door — "That should make him nervous," — then tell Docherty that if he didn't cough up the three grand he was in lumber. "That's when you start to break things," explained Arthur.

"Like what?" asked Terry, in disbelief.

"Terry. We're dealing with a dishonest man here. Perhaps even a dangerous one. We must show him that we mean business."

"In that case I'll knock," said Terry.

fighting in the ring himself a while ago. The girl looked him up and down, observed that it must have been a long time ago, and then went back to her *Telegraph*.

Outside, Arthur was still chuckling at Terry's knockback when a youth carrying one end of a wardrobe backed out of the shop next door and knocked him to the pavement. As Terry helped him to his feet he saw that the youth carrying the wardrobe was Midge.

"You still in this game, Midge?" Arthur asked in surprise as he brushed down his coat and Terry handed him his hat. Midge simply stared at him, popeyed. Arthur reached out, took the Walkman speakers out of Midge's ears and repeated the question. "I would have thought you'd have learned from what happened to me. Still, I suppose it keeps you from sniffing glue on street corners."

"That's right, Mister Daley," said Midge, as the man still holding the other end of the wardrobe told him to hurry up and pick up his end. "I learned a lot from working for you. I'm finking of starting up on my own."

"Oh my good God," chuckled Arthur once they were back in the

Douglas Docherty seemed surprised to see them and seemed a little bewildered as he invited them into the room. "Arthur . . . Terry . . . I didn't expect to see you. I thought that after . . ."

"You thought that after you'd purloined my furniture and flogged it down in Miami that you'd seen the last of me, didn't you, Douglas? People should have told you that it doesn't do to take Arthur Daley for a mug. Either you cough up the six grand you owe me or my friend Mr McCann here goes to work on you. You ready, Terry?"

"Hold on, Arthur," said Terry, embarrassed. "Give the bloke a chance to explain his side of it."

"Thanks, Terry," said Douglas, sitting down on the bed and running his fingers through his hair with his elbows on his knees. He frowned, bit his bottom lip, and looked thoughtful. Then he looked up at Arthur. "I gather you've been taken for a ride," he said.

"You walk off with a container-load of my furniture, six grandsworth, and you call it being taken for a ride?"

"If you're talking about the containers you sent me then you told me they were worth about four grand apiece," said Douglas.

"He told me they were worth three grand," said Terry.

"The rest is for the distress and discomfort you've caused me. Not to mention the damage to my business reputation. Hit him, Terry."

"Leave it out, Arthur, you still ain't given him a chance to explain. Let's hear it then, Douglas."

Douglas took a deep breath and explained. He told them that when the last container had failed to arrive he had done as Arthur had done and checked with the shipping company who had told him that it had been sent to Miami. "I figured you weren't happy with the deal we had, Arthur," he explained. "That there wasn't enough profit in it for you and that you'd got yourself another outlet. So I left and came back over here, looking for someone else to do the buying. Unfortunately I haven't found anyone reliable enough yet."

"I know what you mean," said Arthur, his manner a mixture of sympathy and unallayed suspicion. "It's the pitfall any honest man faces in today's jungle. But if it's not you that's done me up, then . . ."

"Then it was someone from your end, Arthur," said Douglas.

"Maybe it was Midge," said Terry with a chuckle.

"Do me a favour, Terry," said Arthur. "That walking transistor radio hasn't got brains enough to rob his own piggy bank. I even had to show him where to put his X on the shipping forms when the box was full."

"When you what?" asked Douglas.

"When I showed him how to fill out the shipping forms," explained Arthur, feeling a sudden sinking feeling in his wallet, and his self esteem. "He came to me and asked how he should fill in the form when the driver came to take the container away. Said it would save us both time. Said it would . . . oh my good God. Terry, what's the name of that boozer where he and his pals with the multicoloured hair go to get their eardrums battered into submission every Friday?"

Terry told them it was called *The Pegasus* and Arthur told him that they were going over there and that when they got there they were going to string up that ungrateful little toerag from the lamp

post by whatever was handy.

"After all I've done for him, Terence," Arthur complained as Terry drove towards *The Pegasus*. "I give him a start. An apprenticeship in an honourable trade. And he repays me with a knife between the shoulderblades. I want you to make him suffer, Terry."

When they arrived at *The Pegasus*, they saw Midge about to climb onto a large, B registered motorbike. Terry called out to him and when he saw them he made a run for the corner. Terry caught him before he got there. He drew back a fist, but Terry knocked it aside and warned him not to try it. Just then, Arthur arrived, wheezing and puffing and clapping at his chest with the hand that held the cigar. "Explain the situation to him, Terence," he said between breaths.

"No need, Arthur," said Midge with a shrug. "You going to get Tel to give me a good spanking for it?"

"My four grand might just save you from it," said Arthur.

"Three grand," corrected Midge.

"Hold on a minute," said Terry. "Just how much was that furniture worth?"

"I told you, Terry," said Arthur. "Four grand."

"Three," said Midge. "The old crook bunged roundabout an extra grand on every load he sent over. Eight loads. I loaded six of them myself. I reckoned with profits like that he could stand the losses."

"Arthur," said Terry, looking threateningly across to where Arthur was humming and hawing as he searched for an answer, "is he right?"

"Normal business practice in such circumstances, Terry. Perfectly ethical. What the other man doesn't know can't hurt him."

"And even with the missing furniture you've still got to be at least six or seven grand in front."

"There've been expenses, Terry. Overheads. Devaluation of stock. Wear and tear to my nerves as the organiser of the operation . . ."

But once again, Terry wasn't listening to him. He had gone for a drink with Midge in *The Pegasus* where, over the din of electric guitars, Midge explained to him how his brother had gone to Miami on a holiday flight and then sold the furniture in the two weeks that he had been over there. Terry asked him if he'd any of the money left. Midge said that they'd blown it all, then, after another drink, he'd told him that they had just over three grand left. Terry told him that if he gave him a monkey for Arthur and two hundred for himself then he'd put him onto someone who would do business with him for as long as he was honest. When Midge had agreed, Terry told him to take the money that was left and go and see Douglas Docherty and explain how they'd got it. "But will he trust me if he knows how I got it?" asked Midge doubtfully.

"He trusted Arthur, Midge," said Terry. "That means he'll trust anybody."

Unlucky Dip

Arthur has ordered a van load of various goods and Terry has stacked them up in the lock-up. Unfortunately, the crates the goods came in were unmarked, so Arthur has to rely on Terry's memory to find out which crate contains which articles. As Terry hasn't been paid for a week, his memory is understandably hazy. All he is prepared to tell Arthur is:

— The crate with the windscreen wipers is above the one with the glass animals and below the thermal underwear.
— The furry dice are to the right of the glass animals and above the zips.
— The music boxes are below the razor blades and left of the windscreen wipers.
— The water pistols are above the nodding dogs and to the right of the thermal underwear.
— The flip-flops are between the t-shirts and the zips.
— Terry had no idea where the rubber crocodiles were.

Can you find out which crate contains what as fast as Arthur did?

The Umpire Strikes Out

"For the last time," Terry protested vehemently, stopping suddenly as they walked down the dusty, litter-laden street. "I am not going to work in your caff. I've already told you I've got something arranged!"

Arthur looked at him thoughtfully. "Something arranged?" he asked quietly. "That would have gone down well at Dunkirk, that would." Here Arthur imitated Terry's voice. "I'd like to help you, Winston, but I've got something arranged."

Terry stifled an urge to break his neck. "Arthur," he said simply, "I'm not going to do it. You've never really cared about that dump anyway."

"Not while it reaped the small but steady returns my half share entitled me to. But now Tom's laid up with three cracked ribs and the place is under threat from teenage marauders." He peeled five £10 notes from a wad and fanned them out like a magician doing a card trick. "I think five good men should be company enough."

Terry looked at his shoes. His rent was due and he didn't have enough to get his suit back from the cleaners. A small white feather drifted by on the breeze. With some extra money he could fill up his car and still have the nights free to make it up to Sheila. She hadn't been all that keen on the away match at Bournemouth in the first place. "Ten."

Arthur made an irritating clicking noise with his tongue. "You're a hard man, Terence," he said, peeling off another three notes. "We'll say £80 — and you don't have to wear the white cap."

While Arthur drove off to see whether he could off-load six tons of demerera sugar without having to actually collect the stuff, Terry let himself into the cafe through the kitchen.

The place was a mess. The smashed glass door had been boarded up, chairs with their backs broken stuck their legs in the air like dead insects, smashed crockery, still dirty, lay around the floor, an upturned urn bled its last dregs of tea onto the counter, and a thin crust was forming on the strange symbols that had been daubed on the walls in tomato sauce. Terry looked up when he heard a gleaming red Vauxhall Astra pull up outside.

A young man of no more than seventeen climbed out of the driver's seat. His face was white and worried and the tortoiseshell frames for his spectacles had recently been repaired with sticking plaster. He knocked on the hardboard covering the window and Terry let him in. "Need any help?" asked the youth, holding out his hand. "I'm Martin Judd."

"Terry McCann. What had you got in mind?"

Martin looked around the wrecked cafe, then went out to his car and spoke briefly into a radio phone. He kicked the car door shut and came back grinning. "Some of the boys are coming along. They'll soon help us clear this lot up."

"I'm glad of the help," admitted Terry, puzzled. "But can you tell me why you're doing this?"

Martin looked at him as if he was a particularly interesting zoo specimen. "We work here," he explained. "At least we used to before we bought the offices up West. This is where we dreamed up Slalom Kong."

"Oh."

"You know," Martin prompted, miming a monkey at speed, "Slalom Kong — the fastest selling video game last year. The follow-up's out for Christmas. We still come here for inspiration."

Terry laughed as he wiped some of the sauce off the walls. "Do you know what happened?" he asked.

Martin nodded. "We were sitting right there," he began, pointing at a corner table. "Tom was behind the counter. These wallies came in and smashed the place up. I'd never seen them before."

Terry fetched a large rag from the back and began swabbing the floor while Martin stacked any unbroken crockery he could find into the sink. When four of Martin's friends turned up and pitched in with a will, Terry was beginning to think that maybe there was hope for the human race yet.

And then Arthur turned up. "Nice motor out there," he said, surveying the surroundings with disgust. His gaze came to rest on the freshly brewed cup of tea in Martin's hand. "Have you paid for that?" he demanded. Martin shook his head. Arthur wagged his finger. "Terry — throw him out."

"Give it a rest, Arthur. These lads helped —"

Suddenly the door burst open and a crowd of young men, their faces swathed with scarves and balaclavas, came streaming in, shouting at the top of their voices and lashing out with feet and fists. Arthur cowered against the wall, feebly waving a fork in the air as Martin and his pals did what they could against their larger opponents.

Terry put two down and had dived on a third when a chair leg smashed against the back of his head. He pulled himself unsteadily to his feet as one thug head butted him in the stomach and another landed a two-fisted blow on his neck. He shook his head and his hand grabbed the end of a scarf as someone blew a whistle and the cafe began to empty as quickly as it had filled. Terry pulled hard on the scarf and punched the head behind it when it came into range. In return, the chair leg crashed down against his knuckles and rapped him a stinging blow to the ear. Terry let go of the scarf and the man ran out. His colleagues were already piling into Martin's car, spilling papers, a portable typewriter, two cases, a mini-computer and several bags of pear drops.

"Wait here," Terry told Arthur, running for the door. The man with the chair leg was hanging onto the open door of the Astra as it squealed off. Terry jumped at the door as it passed, slamming

the man against the frame. He lost his grip and fell, rolling into the gutter while the car roared off into the distance.

"You're nicked, son," said Terry, walking up to the crumpled figure. Before he got there the man leaped to his feet, hurled the chair leg at him and took off down a narrow alley nearby. Terry gave chase.

The man vaulted the wall at the end of the alley and sprinted through the back door of a launderette. Terry chased him out of the front and across a busy road, cutting through the ranks of a brass band playing on the other side. The man raced through the ground floor of a large store and — after hurling a handful of pick 'n' mix sweets at Terry in desperation — weaved through a crowded shopping mall and dived into the lift of a multi-storey car-park. Terry arrived just as the door was hissing shut. Terry caught the door with both hands and tried to push it back. The man took full advantage, aiming a flurry of punches at Terry's head and arms and kicking him repeatedly in the shin. When the door started opening, Terry stormed into the lift, lifted the man up by the collar of his leather jacket and slammed him backwards against the wall. "Okay, pal," he gasped, pressing the button for the top floor. "You've got ten storeys to tell me yours."

Back at the cafe, Arthur was getting the worst of an argument with Martin.

"I'm holding you responsible," said Martin. "There was two years hard work in that case."

"Work? You?" asked Arthur incredulously. "What are you — a door to door simpleton?"

"I'm the president of the fastest moving company on the stock exchange," said Martin coolly, "and the estimated profits on Slalom Kong 11 alone are expected to pass the seven digit mark."

"Pull the other one. Just leave your money and hop it!" He was lighting his cigar when two schoolboys and a schoolgirl in green blazers came in demanding a cup of tea. Arthur ignored them and then the idea germinated and he suddenly realised a nice brew might be just the ticket. He went into the back, put the kettle on the stove and turned on the gas. When he returned, the crowd had multiplied ten-fold.

"Oi, Curly," shouted one girl, "a bottle of lemonade and two packets of cheese and onion crisps."

"We're closed. Clear off." Arthur dislodged the girl's grip on a jam doughnut and looked round for something to wipe his hands on.

"Snap it up, grandad!" called a bullet-headed pre-teen whose school tie had been severed just below the knot. "I want four strawberry milkshakes and an egg sandwich!"

When he started stuffing his pockets with sugar cubes, Arthur wiped his hands on his head. The boy's neck snapped back and he bit Arthur hard on the back of the hand. As Arthur wondered how soon he would need a tetanus injection, the barrage of demands rioted through his thoughts like drunken monkeys at a seance.

"I've changed my mind! I want the green one."

"I've got this note from my mother. No sugar."

"Where's my yo-yo?"

"Sausage, egg, chips, beans, bacon . . ."

"Green! Green, you wazzock!"

"Someone's nicked my catapult!"

"Water! Water!"

"Liver, mushrooms, tomatoes, gravy . . ."

"Who's got my dosh?"

"Help! I'm stuck!"

"If I'd known it was free I wouldn't have pretended to be sick!"

"I blame the Chinese!"

"Help! Help!"

"Two steak and kidney puddings and a cornish pastie to take out."

"They're the biggest things that ever lived, you know — except for oak trees."

"If you're in a quicksand you've got to lie still."

"Help!"

"And then he puts on this mask and grabs a great big —"

"Shape yourself! We've got to be back in five minutes!"

Arthur felt faint. The hubbub was exhausting his mind. He walked into the back room, put a teabag in a cup, took the kettle from the stone and poured some water on top. He was about to light a cigar when it struck him how strange it was that the kettle was still cold after five minutes on the oven. And then the hissing from the stove reminded him he'd forgotten to light the gas.

Arthur turned off the gas and ran into the other room, coughing and waving his hand in front of his face. "Everybody out!" he ordered, herding the kids to the door. "There's been a gas leak! The whole place could blow up!" He made it to the door and was carried into the street by the flood of kids pouring out. He was trying to wedge the door open with a broken plate when a small man carrying a brief case appeared at his side.

"Are you the proprietor of this establishment?"

"I . . .er . . ." Arthur began coughing again.

The man peered into the cafe. "Perhaps you could help me," he said. "I'm from the Department of Health."

Inside the lift, Terry had learned

all he wanted to know by the seventh floor. Now, his face set with a grim determination, he was running at a crouch for the back door of a large grey, apparently abandoned building.

Terry cautiously made his way up the rubbish-strewn stairs. When he reached the second floor he stepped over a pile of empty boxes and made his way down the corridor, past bulging rubbish bags, a long dry mop standing abandoned in its bucket, a badly dented filing cabinet with its drawers buckled and hanging open, and several cracked and rotting doors that had been torn from their hinges and left where they lay. When he reached a door marked FIRE ESCAPE, he stopped and listened carefully. The tinny whisper of a transistor radio could be heard inside, occasionally drowned by the muffled sound of laughter. Terry picked up a piece of wood and kicked the door open.

There were only three of them left inside, sitting on old mattresses half folded against the walls. All three had cans of beer in their hands. One man threw his can at Terry who used his piece of wood to smash it into the wall. A second man came forward swinging, and as Terry squared up to him, the one who'd thrown the can bolted past him out of the door. Terry parried a right hook with his stick, ducked under a wild left, and dumped the man on the seat of his pants with a right he could feel all the way down to his toes. The last man climbed out of the window and started running down the fire escape. Terry was after him in a flash, vaulting the railings and landing on the fleeing vandal's back. They rolled down the rusty steps and crashed into the weatherbeaten railings. Terry heard a scream and the snapping of eroded metal and reached out blindly. A strong fist grabbed his forearm and suddenly Terry found himself lying face down on the fire escape with the thief swinging on his arm above a twenty-foot drop. "Hold on," urged Terry, gripping the arm tighter as he struggled to his knees.

The thug used his free hands to draw a knife. "You're not taking me in," he threatened, snarling up at Terry's face.

Terry couldn't believe his ears. "If you had a brain, you'd be dangerous," he said. "Touch me with that knife and I'm letting go." The thug looked down at the hard cobble stones below then back up at Terry. Terry smiled as the thug dropped the knife. "That's it, Einstein — we're going to have a talk."

The arrival of both the Fire Brigade and Detective Sergeant Chisholm at the cafe had done nothing to improve Arthur's temper. The fact that Chisholm only stayed long enough to pass a few unkind comments about Arthur's predicament was offset by the smirks on the firemen's faces, the constant haranguing from Martin and his pals, and the insistent murmuring of the man from the Department of Health. When Terry pulled up in Martin's Astra Arthur took the opportunity of shrugging off the man's attentions and walked over to greet him. He was surprised to see that Tom was driving and that Terry was in the back with one of the hooligans that had wrecked the cafe. Terry climbed out of the car and dragged the vandal after him by the scruff of his neck. Arthur stepped forward angrily and aimed a slap at him.

"That's enough, Arthur," Terry ordered, letting the thief loose. "This fellah's got something to tell you about your mutual friend, Toerag Tommy."

Tom climbed out of the car looking sheepish. "I did my best, Arthur," he protested, grinning shamefacedly. "The caff wasn't paying enough. Then I had big business on one side and light fingered mobs of demented sub-humans on the other — it was all I could do to keep the peace. My role was more one of umpire than agent provocateur."

"What's he babbling about?"

"He stitched you up good and proper," Terry explained. "When he found out that the council wanted this land for development, he ran the business down so he could buy you out cheap and sell to them at a fat profit."

"And when that didn't work," the vandal butted in, "he got a few of us to close you down for him."

"You mean you faked those rib injuries?" asked Arthur. "My own partner? Tom, I'm lost for words. You're the lowest, filthiest, greediest —"

"I did have a bad chest," offered Tom in his defence. "And I *was* very tired."

"Tired? You'll be six feet under if you don't immediately sign your half over to me for a nominal sum."

"You mean like a gentleman's agreement?" asked Tom.

Arthur snorted. "I mean legal and binding — right now."

Martin walked up as Arthur handed Tom a pencil and an old betting slip to write on. "Where's Slalom Kong 11?" he asked the hooligan.

"What?"

"That little black case that was inside the car," Martin explained. Terry noticed Arthur sidling up to the boot of his car. "Maybe Arthur can help you!" he said, very loudly.

Arthur scowled. "You mean that funny looking little case that was lying in the street?" he asked, surprised. "Now I think of it, I do remember picking up something or other in all the confusion. You can't be too careful these days, can you?"

"Not with you around," muttered Terry.

Arthur was unloading the computer and the case containing Slalom Kong 11 when the man from the Department of Health put his hand on Arthur's shoulder and waved the betting slip in his face. "Now that you appear to be the sole owner of this establishment," he smiled, "perhaps we could talk about the improvements that will have to be made."

Arthur sat on the edge of his car seat with his feet on the pavement. "Terry, how much would you want for sorting out this bureaucratic dictator?"

"Knock it on the head, Arthur."

Arthur gazed long and hard at the man from the Department of Health, then swung his legs inside the car. "Ah, well . . ."

"'Ang on a mo'," Martin complained. "Where's my bloomin' pear drops?"

THREE-TIME LOSERS

Arthur and Terry are late for a car auction where Arthur wants to bid for an old banger he thinks has been fitted with a new, super-charged engine. But Plod's on the prowl for hookey gear, and Arthur is a likely suspect to put in the frame. That's why he and Terry keep getting stopped, and every time they do, they get a little later for the auction. Could you get there in time? Find out by playing this game. Don't be a three-time loser. Stop once at a "Plod" square and you miss a turn. Stop twice, and you miss two turns. Stop three times and you've had your chips — it's right back to the start. The winner is the first player to reach the auction with an exact throw.

PRINCESS ~CRAZY~

"I will never give in to blackmail!" shrieked the newspaper seller, clutching Arthur's money to her chest. "I'd rather die first! Lock me away if you must! I'll do my cornflakes. A little bit of budgie won't hurt me. In my own country I am a princess!"

Arthur backed nervously away from the woman. She stood a little over four feet tall and was carrying a plastic bag with NEWSPAPERS written on the side with a green felt tip pen.

"I'm not talking about blackmail," said Arthur. "This is daylight robbery." He held his magazine in the air. "I asked for a *Financial Times* and you gave me a brochure on how to make model aeroplanes. There's not even any bingo!"

"So?" asked the woman defiantly.

"It was printed in January 1964," Arthur went on. "It's not going to look too good in the office if all I've got to feed into the computer is an outdated list of glue prices and a picture of a plastic dive-bomber."

"Turn it in, Arthur," said Terry, waiting beside Arthur. "You haven't got a computer. Or an office. You just want to be seen carrying a serious newspaper as a front for this deal you've got lined up." He took the magazine and handed it back to the woman. "Haven't you got anything more suitable, Princess? Like a colouring book?"

"You'll get nothing from me!" the woman cried, snatching the magazine and putting it in her bag.

She pulled out a large, ragged dandelion. "Unless you want to buy some lucky heather."

"Terry — it's your duty to recover my money!"

"Do me a favour," said Terry, walking off.

Arthur scooted after him. "Terry! That was a pound note I gave her!"

Terry ignored him and led the way over a metal bridge spanning a canal. Below them, brightly decorated narrowboats lined each bank.

"Right then, which one is it?" asked Terry when they reached the other side.

Arthur looked up and down the row of boats. "Hang on a minute . . . that's it. That black one up there. *Blossom*."

Terry's gaze followed Arthur's pointing finger. "The one with the dog?"

Arthur's face grew increasingly worried as they neared the boat. He looked up and down the row of boats again, then sighed. "That's it," he confirmed wearily. "The one with the dog."

Arthur and Terry eyed the huge alsatian blocking the short gangplank onto the narrowboat with suspicion. When the dog started barking at them Arthur pushed Terry forward. "You know the saying, Terry — a barking dog never bites."

"You mean a biting dog can't bark as well," said Terry, stepping forward and raising his hand. "Sit!"

The dog stared at him with its head on one side and its tongue hanging out, then turned and loped up the gangplank onto the boat. Terry and Arthur were following when the door to the cabin popped open and a bearded, beaming face emerged.

"Mr Daley — so pleased you could make it. Come in while I put the kettle on."

Arthur, Terry and the dog went into the narrowboat. They sat down and the man fixed Terry with a penetrating gaze. "Scorpio, right?"

"Terry McCann."

The man handed out mugs of tea and then stood in front of the small stove with his legs apart and his hands purposefully clenched behind his back. "My name's Ruperts, Terry. As I was telling Arthur in the pub, I'm something of a student . . . a student of the unknown."

"Oh." Terry sipped his tea.

Arthur moved away from the dog.

"You see, Terry, whether we like it or not, every single one of us — either consciously or unconsciously — is vitally affected by the unknown. But, despite our continued fascination with the subject, very little is actually known about the unknown."

"I didn't know that."

"Mr Ruperts is an artist, Terry," said Arthur, by way of an explanation. "Like you."

Terry did a double take as Arthur turned away and patted the dog.

"Exactly," Ruperts confirmed, throwing the dog a biscuit. "Marvellous animal, the dog. Don't you agree? Nature at her most inventive. Note how the tail is curved to allow the fleas to loop the loop."

Terry rolled his eyes and stared at the ceiling.

"Mr Ruperts has been offered a contract in Hollywood," said Arthur, frowning disapprovingly at Terry's behaviour. "Set designer. That's why he has to sell the boat."

"Right!" smiled Ruperts, taking an open tin of beans from the cupboard and pouring them onto a saucer for the dog. "And with money no longer a problem, I want only the best for my boat. I need someone sensitive to have it, someone who will treat it right. In short, someone like you, Terry — an artist, a man of character."

"Just a minute," began Terry. "I'm not sure — "

"Don't be so proud, Terence," Arthur interrupted. "I've said that I'll make you a loan until you're on your feet. It's only right that those of us who've carved ourselves a slice should help you others of a more caring, noble nature."

"I couldn't have put it better myself," agreed Ruperts, filling the empty saucer with milk. "I believe £750 was the agreed deposit?"

Arthur kicked the dog gently when it ignored the milk and began sniffing his turn-ups.

"£750 it was, Mr Ruperts," said Arthur, getting out his cheque book. The dog bounded over to Ruperts and put its paws on his chest.

"Cash."

"Of course, of course," muttered Arthur, a sickly look on his face. "You do have a bill of sale?" He counted the money out on the table.

"Everything above board and shipshape, Mr Daley," said Ruperts, exchanging a densely typed document for the thick wad of bills.

"Well, I'll leave you to it then," smiled Arthur, winding his watch. "Must dash."

Terry stood up, grabbed Arthur's shoulder and marched him through the door.

"Off the cloth," said Arthur when they got outside. "Remember you're supposed to be sensitive."

The alsatian followed them out and sat down, panting.

"You'll be bloomin' sensitive if you don't tell me what's going on," growled Terry.

"It's simple. I met raving Ruperts in a pub and he said he was looking for a buyer for his barge. Said he wanted someone with a creative bent."

"Why?"

"I've already told you, Terry. He's intelligent." Arthur pointed to his temple with his index finger and made a rotating movement. Terry let go of his coat. Arthur smiled sympathetically. "Just make sure he doesn't run off with my investment."

"Where's he going to go?" asked Terry. "Those things have got a top speed of about 5 mph."

"I don't care. You keep an eye on it. I'll be back later."

The dog followed him ten yards down the towpath then settled down and went to sleep.

Terry walked to a pub at the side of the canal. He bought a half of lager and settled down in a window seat with a good view of *Blossom*. He was finishing his drink when three motorcyclists, dressed in black leather and carrying staves, screeched to a halt by the boat. Terry put down his glass and was out of the door in time to see Ruperts wrestle one of the men to the floor. The other two were busy smashing the boat's windows.

When Terry reached the boat the nearest man rushed him, the stave held high above his head. Terry grabbed it as it came down, pulled the man's arm over his shoulder as he went into a turn, and used the man's own momentum to send him somersaulting through the air and landing flat on his back on the towpath. As he picked up the stave, Terry heard Ruperts' stangled voice warning him to watch out.

The roar of a powerful motorcycle sounded and Terry turned. The other attacker had remounted his machine and was now letting out the clutch as he surged directly at Terry. Terry stepped to the edge of the canal, and as the bike hurtled towards him, he jumped back on the towpath and swung the stave like a baseball bat. He caught the man on the back of his gleaming black helmet and the bike reared up on its back wheel, kicking up dirt as it wobbled dangerously close to the still, black water. Then the front wheel slammed down, the rider gained control, and the bike sped past two startled ducks and onto the open road.

Terry heard a splash and saw Ruperts' yellow trousers disappearing into the murky canal waters. Terry jumped on the attacker's back and grabbed him round the throat as the dog jumped up and down beside them, snapping and snarling. The man stumbled to his knees and Terry did a forward roll, turned fast, grabbed the man's arm and banged it against his knee. He dropped his stave and Terry heard a muffled cry inside the helmet. He pushed the man roughly onto the strip of grass that separated the towpath from a strip of road.

"Off with the helmet," he ordered. The man obeyed. Terry's eyes went skywards when the ruffled features were exposed. "Andy!" he groaned. "I thought you'd packed this caper in."

"You know how it is, Tel," said Andy, rubbing his bruised arm. "Times are tight."

"Don't give me the sob story. Last I heard you had a job at the bakery."

"I had to pack it in, Terry. It was too hot. There were all these ovens. And I kept having nightmares about sliced bread. Armies of the stuff. All lined up in ranks and — "

Terry shook his head in dismay and let go of his grip on Andy's collar. The dog closed in, growling.

"It wasn't anything personal, Tel," Andy apologised from the floor. "I didn't know you had anything to do with this boat. The bloke that owns it owes my gaffer five grand."

Out of the corner of his eye, Terry caught sight of Ruperts' muddy head ducking into the narrowboat cabin. "You mean Ruperts?" he asked.

Arthur was crossing the metal bridge.

"Not Ruperts," Andy explained. "This boat belongs to Gordon Wallace."

"Never heard of him." Terry turned to face Arthur.

"Brilliant," said Arthur sarcastically, as he looked over the damage. Ruperts' grinning face peeped out of a smashed window and asked him if he wanted a cup of tea. Arthur ignored him and continued his tirade. "A really first class job, Terry. I don't know why I bother to pay you — I really don't. Is this the one?" He pointed at Andy. "You little git." Arthur pulled back his foot as if to kick him. Andy cowered. The dog barked. Down the towpath the pub had closed and a handful of men were walking past.

One of them, a tiny man with Captain Kirk sideburns and ears Spock wouldn't have sneezed at, grabbed Arthur by the arm. "You look like a sensible man," he said. "You've got lucky eyes. Have you got £5 to give me?"

"No."

The man took out a small snuff tin with the sides flattened crudely. "Go on, £5 and it's yours. You put a little water in it, add sand for weight, bung it in freezer and bingo — you've got a 50p piece that would fool any machine. And if you wrap it in silver paper, I can tell you the name of a shop where the assistant's eyes aren't too sharp. I'd keep it for myself but I can't find a plug for my fridge."

Arthur was trying to tear himself free when a white Rolls Royce pulled up on the narrow strip of road next to the footpath. A man who Arthur recognised as Nifty Ned Charnley got out of the front door in a badly fitting chauffeur's uniform and opened the back door. He held it open while a small woman dressed in red, with a white fur stole and a gleaming tiara stepped out. Even without the shopping bag and the dandelion, Arthur and Terry could immediately tell it was Princess, the newspaper girl. Behind her a middle aged man in a sober suit came out. Princess was stepping daintily down to the towpath when she caught sight of the smashed windows. Her eyes darted from side to side as if in panic, then she walked up to Arthur and kissed him on the cheek. "Don't make it hard on yourself," she said loudly.

"It's over. It cannot be. Monte Carlo was just an aberration. In Ibiza, I was carried away by the sunsets. Rome was madness. The wine, the song, the gentle lapping of the tide, the gondolas — forgive me, but I love another!"

Arthur pushed her away and brushed down his suit. The alsatian ran round in circles, barking at its tail. The man in the sober suit came up and shook Arthur by the hand. "John Stoddard. I've asked Princess to marry me. No hard feelings, eh?"

Arthur eyed him suspiciously. Terry came up and hustled him into the cabin on the narrowboat. The dog followed. Ruperts was pouring some water into a kettle. "Sugar?" he asked.

Terry seemed exasperated. "You've got some explaining to do."

Ruperts glanced out of the window and saw Andy, Princess and Stoddard talking happily. "I suppose you're right. I didn't really want to involve you, anyway. It seemed so logical at first."

"Funny how things turn out," said Terry pointedly.

Ruperts sat down. "Princess is my mum," he explained. "Stoddard is my dad. They grew up together in Rochdale. Princess wouldn't marry him at the time, so when she ran off down here he married someone else. They still kept in touch, though, and when Stoddard said in his letters how well he was doing in his carpet business Princess would answer saying she was doing better. She's always regretted letting him go, you see. Theirs was a classical love, a brief flame—"

"Knock off the Barbara Cartland," said Arthur. "Where's my money?"

"Anyway," Ruperts continued, "Stoddard's wife upped and left him after thirty-six years of marriage. Ran off with a butcher from Oldham. And when he wrote saying he was coming down to see her we thought if we hired a Roller and got some fancy clothes he'd be impressed. And then Gordon Wallace said he was going away for a few days and we asked if we could borrow the boat."

"This boat isn't yours?" asked Arthur, like a teacher trying to make sense of a particularly devious excuse.

Ruperts beamed. "It's not technically mine, no," he admitted.

"You're nothing but a con man!" Arthur rebuked him. Terry smiled.

"When I heard you say you were looking for a narrowboat it seemed too good an opportunity to miss. I pretended to be an artist and you fell for it. You thought I was stupid, there for the taking, a mug, a dreamer, an idiot, a mark—"

"Where's my money?" Arthur repeated.

Ruperts fished in the pocket of his soaking wet trousers and pulled out a roll of soggy bills. "I'll need a tenner for Nifty Ned and the windows will cost about—"

Arthur snatched the money from his hand and began counting it. The alsatian howled.

Outside, John Stoddard had produced some sparkling wine from the car and a small party was getting underway. Terry congratulated the happy couple and after a quick glass of wine he went to join Arthur, who was pacing angrily back and forth at the foot of the metal bridge. They were halfway across the bridge when Ruperts' voice carried to them across the water. "Arthur! Terry! Aren't you going to take your dog with you?"

SLENDER MERCIES

"So you see, Mr Daley, as executors of the deceased's estate, we here at Murcheson, Haynes and Cartwright have a responsibility to locate the whereabouts of the sole heir — in this instance, one James Hardwick Ibbotson."

Arthur nodded at Mr Murcheson and stole a glance at some squash rackets in the corner, mentally checking their quality against the genuine rubberette ones he had back at the warehouse.

"Of course there will be a substantial finder's fee involved," Murcheson continued, handing Arthur a faded photograph of a man in army uniform. "And we shall be looking to you to act with the utmost discretion in this delicate matter."

"Of course," agreed Arthur, eyeing the thick strands of rust red hair, dragged like seaweed across the freckled pate. He wondered whether it was the right time to mention the gross of 'supa-tuff' ready to wear drip dry toupees he had in the car outside. "Just exactly how substantial is substantial?" he asked cagily.

Murcheson smiled and indicated the opulent surroundings of his office. "Take it from me, Mr Daley, if you find Mr Hardwick for us you will be more than pleased with your fee. And in the meantime, of course, you'll have the £300 expenses."

Arthur remembered the money in his pocket and got up to leave. "It's been a pleasure, Mr Murcheson," he said, shaking hands. "I'll be in touch the moment we contact Mr Hardwick."

"Have you thought any more about those shares?" asked Murcheson pleasantly. "I don't think they can keep the lid on their new process much longer. And the computer projects for the 1988 cocoa crops make a merger seem imminent."

"Yes, I know," lied Arthur, opening the door. "My man in Japan reports personally every week."

He left the office and went down to the street where Terry was waiting for him in the Jag. "I've got a job for you," he said, pushing Terry over to the passenger seat. "Find Smelly Ibbotson."

James Hardwick Ibbotson, known to all as Smelly, was a tall, whippet thin man who, if you could get close enough to focus properly, had looked to be on the verge of death ever since his teens. Now, sixty-seven years old, his only other noticeable achievements were that he rarely spoke and during the summer months could be found sitting in doorways reading and re-reading a tattered tract entitled *Obfuscation in International Morality*. He was occasionally adopted as a referee by a man known as the Colonel, whose squabbles with a lady named Tiger Millie often went on for months. Nobody knew where Smelly went in winter.

Terry caught up with the Colonel and Tiger Millie that evening. They were sitting round a makeshift fire on some waste ground, gazing glassy eyed into the flames. As Terry walked up he was surprised to see a half empty picnic hamper and some empty bottles of champagne. The Colonel and Millie were eating sandwiches and Terry grew slightly disturbed at the sight of Millie's garish

new makeup and the huge false eyelashes half hanging from her lids.

"How's it going then?" he asked.

The Colonel ignored him. Millie glared.

"I still say it's caviare," said the Colonel, rubbing his false teeth on the sleeve of his coat. "It's not a taste you can easily forget."

"It's ham," insisted Millie, peeking under the crust. "You can tell by the veins of fat."

"Fat doesn't come in veins," the Colonel asserted. "If it's not caviare it must be bloater paste."

"Looks nice," lied Terry.

The Colonel seemed to be seeing him for the first time. "Go away," he said courteously. "As we told the others, we are men of honour. We shall never, ever, talk . . . for less than a monkey, at least."

"I don't know what you're talking about." Terry was getting confused.

Millie stood up and hurled a shoe at him. It caught him a glancing blow on the forehead. "That's enough of that," he warned. Millie sat down heavily and one of her false eyelashes fell into her cup. She put her hand in to try and fish it out and the contents of the cup spilled out onto her sandwiches.

The colonel picked up a large stone. "Your 'ook," he said menacingly.

"What?"

"Your 'ook. Sling it," Millie joined in. She emptied her cup and took another bite of her sandwich. Her face took on a peculiar expression as she chewed.

"Calm down now," said Terry. "I'm looking for Smelly Ibbotson."

"If it's ham it's very fizzy," murmured Millie, still chewing.

"Smelly Ibottson?" Terry prompted. "I said I'm looking for him."

"Who isn't?" asked the Colonel, tipping up his cup and curling out his tongue to catch the last drop. "You weren't here when we needed you though, were you? Go on, you nosey little git, take your horrible self away from here."

Terry thought of the hundreds of cups of tea he had bought them. He was trying to think of something to say when Millie threw her empty cup at him. It sailed over his shoulder and exploded against an empty fridge. "Go and find him!" she snarled.

The Colonel stood stiffly to attention by her side. "That's right!" he shrieked, his face the colour of an over ripe plum. "Find the cove! And then tell him that we never want to see him again!"

"And that's an order!" Millie howled, picking up another stone.

Terry turned and walked away.

As he picked his way through the mess of broken vacuum cleaners, burnt out chairs and empty tins Terry saw the familiar figure of Rockabilly Rene, shuffling back

from the local library with her three black plastic bags slung over her shoulder. She smiled when she recognised Terry. "I see the two musketeers are still looking for trouble," she said, nodding over Terry's shoulder at the wasteland.

Terry shook his head and wiped the dirt off the bruise forming on his forehead. "Yeah. Too much pop. What do you know?"

"I know who you're looking for. I don't know why."

"Smelly's come into some money," Terry explained.

Rene laughed. "He's come into some money all right — look!" She opened her bag to reveal six frozen chickens and a bottle of cider. "Want a swig?"

Terry shook his head.

Rene's voice grew soft. "I know you'll see he doesn't get hurt."

"If I don't know where he is, I can't help him, can I?"

Rene leaned forward and pushed a crumpled £20 note into his hand. "Smelly was always fond of Southend," she whispered.

Terry stuffed the note back in her bag. "Thanks, Rene. We'll have a drink when I get back."

"You can count on it."

"I don't like it," said Terry as he steered the Jag through the rain towards Southend. Arthur studied the piece of paper in his hand. "I don't like it, either," he mumbled, shaking his head. "You need a bloomin' degree to get yourself robbed these days." He held up the paper and read aloud. "'For locating, supplying, rendering and installing a vehicle propellant reservoir access-closing component . . . £20'."

"Sounds expensive," said Terry. "What does it mean?"

"Fitting a petrol cap, that's what it means. It was a bad day for the motor trade when your university mob moved in. You expect a bit of embellishment from estate agents, but petrol pumpers? I mean . . ."

"What I mean," Terry said, forcing Arthur back on the subject, "is that I don't like this Smelly business. If those lawyers want to find him to give him some money, how come all his pals are rolling in the stuff already?"

"Forget it, Terence," said Arthur airily. "You worry too much. Maybe Murcheson put someone else on the case just to be sure. You just be ready to hump those metal detectors. Then when you've finished, have a quick look under the pier. That way, we've discharged our duty with integrity."

"How do you know Murcheson is a real lawyer?" Terry persisted.

"Of course he's a real lawyer. He plays squash. He's got a gold watch and hairs on the back of his wrist. The man was oozing legality. He could strut sitting down. And he gave me a card."

"Cards are cheap," said Terry, guiding the Jag round a stationary van and stopping at the back of a sea front shop. The rain had stopped and the sun came briefly out.

Terry loaded the metal detectors as Arthur haggled with the shop owner over the price of 2,000 watch batteries. When Arthur went off to see about the franchise for his new line in floating wallets, Terry grabbed a cup of tea, then went in search of Smelly.

He checked out the park, the pier and the fairground, and was working his way systematically through the amusement arcades when some insistent country and western music drifting across from the beach finally claimed his attention. He saw the music came from two men and two women, with the help of a pedal steel, a bass, an organ and a drum. They provided the backdrop to a sparsely attended beauty contest. Six girls in buckskin bikinis and cowboy boots were waiting expectantly while a man in a ten gallon hat took up a sash from the formica table he was sitting behind and walked slowly over to the mike. Rather unnecessarily holding his hands up for quiet, he slowly began reading out numbers from a piece of lined notepaper. Suddenly the girls began shrieking and jumping up and down with glee. Terry was turning to go when one of them rushed sobbing from the group and plopped herself down sadly in front of him on the sand.

"What's the matter?" asked Terry, crouching down with his elbow on his knee.

The girl looked up and smiled bravely through her tears. "I'm sorry," she gulped. "It's just that he promised me a place in the first three if he could take me out to dinner."

"Who?"

"Hank Rio. The one with the stupid hat."

Terry looked across at the sole cowboy judge, who was now mingling with the contestants. Hank Rio, dressed in black boots and trousers, with a string tie clipped loosely round the neck of his black and purple shirt, was kissing the runner-up while helping the winner into a new fur coat. Underneath the ten gallon hat, a familiar face was cracked wide in a hungry smile. Terry walked over. "Mind if I have a word, Mr Ibbotson?" he whispered quietly, tapping him on the shoulder. The cowboy's face froze in fear then just as suddenly relaxed when he saw it was Terry. He kissed the beauty queen on the cheek and told her to wait in his car.

"Surprised you recognised me,

Tel," said Smelly. "Especially with my new store boughts." He grinned again and Terry saw a glistening set of over-large teeth.

"I want to talk to you."

"I want to talk to you, Tel. But not now. Meet me at *The Excelsior* in half an hour."

"It's urgent," Terry insisted.

As Smelly began to remonstrate, two men in dark blue suits stepped out of the thin crowd and grabbed him by the arms. "Back off and you'll get your money," hissed one at Terry.

Smelly dug his elbow back and stamped down with the heel of his hand-tooled cowboy boots. The two men loosened their grip on him and as Smelly turned on them, the one on the left reached inside his pocket. Terry waded in and knocked him back with an uppercut that caught him flush on the jaw. Smelly pulled his Colt 45 Peacemaker replica from his holster and brought the barrel down smartly on the other's head. As the man sank slowly to the sand, Smelly blew some imaginary smoke from the barrel, twirled the blank-firing metal model expertly round his index finger and replaced it in his (authentically) fringed simulated leather-substitute holster. "Never had you figured as a sidewinder, Tel," he began in injured tones.

Terry grabbed him by the elbow and pointed him towards the road. "We're in trouble," he said. "And you're the one who's going to get us out of it."

Three hours later, after a whispered phone call to Arthur, Terry and Smelly were waiting in a muddy quarry while their hired van stood under some nearby trees.

"What's he up to?" Smelly asked Terry, looking at his watch. "Do you think something's happened? He's nearly an hour late."

Terry shrugged and turned his collar up against the rain. He was blowing on his hands when Arthur's Jag came bumping down the quarry's dirt road. It came to a halt about twenty yards from them and Arthur staggered out of the back door. His clothes were filthy and looked wet. He stumbled towards them with one hand raised.

"Terry . . . Terry . . ." His voice trailed off as he fell face forward into an orange coloured puddle. Smelly saw the muscles in Terry's cheek start going.

The other three doors of the Jag opened and slowly, each one dealing a sharp blow to Smelly's confidence, five large men got out and stood facing them. Smelly immediately recognised one of them as Stu Malone, a one time nine stone weakling who several years ago had urged Smelly to join the new revolutionary political party he was forming. Smelly had refused and, as he remembered to his dismay, advised him to get some weights. Murcheson walked forward and rolled Arthur's limp body over with his foot. "The money's all we want," he said. "Give us that and you can go free."

"The police have got the money," said Terry. "It's all over. Go home. Your big mistake was bringing me and Arthur into it."

Murcheson smiled. "Our big mistake was hiding the money in a derelict house when police sealed off the area. But if you think I believe your story you're more stupid than I thought."

"I'm ashamed of you, Stu," called Smelly, ignoring Murcheson. "I never thought you'd stoop this low." Terry was surprised to see Stu shifting uncomfortably. "You could have been someone, Stu — and now look at you. A bully. A crook. A cheap hoodlum. You're scum, Stu, and I'm ready for you. All of you!" His mouth set in a thin line and his bony fingers hovered over the ivory coloured plastic handles of his phoney 45s.

Stu was the first into action. To

everyone's surprise, he ran forward and smacked Murcheson on the back of the head. Murcheson turned and kicked at him and the two men fell to the ground, kicking and punching. Smelly and Terry took this as their signal to go in and while Terry ducked and jabbed, keeping two of the remaining men fully occupied, Smelly laid into his adversary with the butt of his fake hardware. Then Stu finally decked Murcheson with a haymaker right, and the odds swung against the bad guys. Within minutes, three of them were making a run for it while Murcheson struggled to get to his feet, tottered round in circles for a while, then fell flat on his back.

Terry picked Arthur up. His clothes were filthy and soaking wet. There was a small bruise under his eye. His cigar had gone out. Terry dragged him to the van, took off Arthur's wet clothes, then wrapped him in a blanket. He asked Stu to take Arthur's car and then he and Smelly got in the front seat.

"I suppose it's only right to hand the money back," said Smelly glumly as they drove through the night.

Terry smiled. "Of course it's right. And don't forget, you'll get a reward."

"There won't be much of that left when you take out what I've spent. I had plans, Terry. With you as my protector and Arthur as my financial adviser we could have gone places."

"With Arthur as your financial adviser," smiled Terry, pulling up at some lights, "you couldn't have got out of sight."

In the back, Arthur had finally come round. In the darkness of the van, he had no idea where he was. He flung the blanket to one side, opened the back doors to the van and, dressed only in his underpants, stepped bewilderedly out. And then the lights changed and Terry and Smelly drove off. Arthur was left alone in the night, lost and confused, wandering barefoot on the road. A low groan escaped his lips and for a moment it looked as though he might burst into tears. But then he saw the van's brakelights go on, and heard the engine reversing.

Terry climbed out, crossed the road and put his jacket round Arthur's shoulders. "Nearly lost you there, mate," he said, leading Arthur back to the van. "Now what do you say we take you somewhere for some hot food and a good drink?"

Arthur smiled weakly. He was so relieved that for a split second he almost said thanks.

Once upon a time up West

"Ah, yes, a touch of the Casablancas," said Arthur admiringly as he surveyed what Harry from Barry was doing to the *Old Turk's Head* on the corner of Rydal Road. "The mysteries of ancient Egypt and the romance of Hollywood. It's bound to appeal. Very tasteful, Harry, very chic."

A joiner was nailing sheets of hardboard over the inside of the pub's windows then cutting the shapes of tall Moorish windows into them with a jigsaw. An electrician was wiring up a large overhead paddle fan, and two of Harry from Barry's burly business associates — the same two who had collected Arthur that morning from his car lot — were carrying small potted palms through the front doors.

"I suppose you're going to have Barbados Eric on the ivories and waitresses in baggy trousers and curled up slippers bashing out cheeseburgers and funny coloured drinks?"

"Right first time, Arthur," said the little Welsh villain with pride. "My own idea. I've applied to the licensed victualler's board to have the name changed to *Rick's Bar.*"

"Very original, Harry," said Arthur, still shaking his head with admiration. "And if I may make so bold as to say so, very wise. It takes more than pickled eggs and a Friday night raffle to prise your average punter out from the warm cosy glow of his television set. Providing such an attractive and elegant ambience must have stood you in for a tidy sum, Harry. Perhaps I can interest you in a very reasonably priced line in kitchen condiments?"

"Still the same old seedy boyo, eh, Arthur," said Harry. "Trade and barter, duck and dive. As a matter of fact I've a small matter of business I want to discuss."

"I wondered when you had your staff pick me up at the lot whether it was social," said Arthur, swallowing nervously. "Not that I don't appreciate it. I'm always one to appreciate the personal touch."

"Well, Arthur," said Harry in a voice of apologetic explanation, "I thought you might tell me you weren't in if I tried phoning."

"A pointed remark, Harry, but less than fair. When did Arthur Daley ever refuse Harry from Barry a favour?"

"So far you never have, Arthur," said Harry with an appreciative chuckle.

Harry Evans had come to London from Barry as a promising welterweight more than thirty years ago. After a brief career in the ring — his record had been two victories, one defeat, and eight disqualifications — both he and boxing's board of control had decided his talent would best be exercised elsewhere. Once unleashed upon the less carefully regulated world of free enterprise, this talent, allied to Welsh cunning, had succeeded in bringing him considerable wealth, to which age, family life, and a very slippery brief had succeeded in adding some small degree of respectability. Over the years, his manner, which Arthur remembered as once being one of barely controlled aggression, had mellowed gradually into one of magnanimous menace.

"So far you never have," he repeated, producing two cigars

from a box on the bar top and handing one to Arthur. He waited for one of his business associates to provide a light before he spoke again. "But just in case you're thinking of starting, I thought I'd better establish the fact that you owe me."

"Owe you?" asked Arthur, coughing out a half swallowed billow of cigar smoke. "Didn't I persuade that Bengali gent to set his seven daughters' fingers working to run you up a very nice line in après ski lounging pyjamas when your Stella decided she'd like to try her hand at the fashion game? And didn't I buy back what you had left when she decided she'd had enough of cut price haute couture?"

"That you did, Arthur, and I've always appreciated the gesture. You saved my Stella a lot of undue worry. And, as I recall, you gave me a very fair price for them."

"As I recall, I didn't have much option," said Arthur despondently as he remembered how long they had been stacked up in his lock-up before Terry had had the bright idea of knocking them out at not far from cost to the local martial arts club. Arthur still had nightmares in which granite handed karate dans in pink satin lounging pyjamas pursued him round Fulham demanding satisfaction. "And what about the foam-backed Persian rugs?"

"No complaints there, either, Arthur," acknowledged Harry. "It was that business with the pinball machines I was thinking of."

"An innocent enough misunderstanding, Harry, of the kind that could happen to anyone. If you cast your mind back I'm sure you'll recollect that you stopped payment on the cheque and put the lot through a car crusher before Inspector Ryecott arrived making his customary ill conceived and untoward enquiries."

"I know that, Arthur," agreed Harry, nodding to himself at Arthur's words. "But technically speaking I still owe you a good going over for selling them to me in the first place. After all, I do have my reputation to think of nowadays."

"Ah, I see what you're driving at, Harry," said Arthur with some relief. "But you can rest assured I shall remain mutton on the subject."

"Glad you can look at it so sensibly, Arthur," said Harry with a smile. "I like a man with such a keen sense of where his best interests lie. There's something I want you to do for me."

"I thought there might be," said Arthur gloomily. Then, noticing the air of self congratulation with which Harry was smoking his cigar, he added, "Of course, whenever we've established just what it is you have in mind, Harry, perhaps we could discuss a fee."

When Harry from Barry had told Arthur what he wanted from him, and Harry's accountant and personnel manager had dropped Arthur back at the car lot from which they had removed him that morning, Arthur made a quick phone call to Soupy Sturridge, went to visit a West End jewellery store, then decided to seek out Terry.

As Arthur had bunged him a ton the previous afternoon for his part in retrieving one of Arthur's motors from a local chancer whose cheque had bounced higher than the top storey of his re-

cently repossessed house in the stockbroker belt, Terry didn't prove that hard to find. He was still in bed.

"Terry, the streets are full of folk who've been engaged in life's hurly burly for almost half a day already," said Arthur disapprovingly as Terry, dressed only in his jeans, undid the chain and let him in.

"Yeah, I know about that," said Terry, rubbing a knuckle into the hollow of his eye as Arthur walked past. "What are you doing round here so early?"

"Your friend Kev McKeown, Terry — he still at the same gaff?" asked Arthur as Terry switched on the kettle and disappeared into the bathroom.

"Yeah, unless he lost it in a card game," said Terry, reappearing in a shirt then making two coffees. "What do you want to find Kev McKeown for, anyway?"

Arthur asked Terry if he had something a little stronger to put in it. Terry asked him sarcastically if he'd had a hard morning sitting in his caravan down the car lot.

"Listen, Terence," protested Arthur indignantly, "while you've been chasing Bo Derek round the daffodils in the land of nod, I've been having a very traumatic experience with Harry from Barry."

"Harry from Barry. You *are* living dangerously. How is he?"

"Same as ever," said Arthur. "Plenty of clout and no idea what to do with it. He wanted the SP on your mate Kevin and his fondness for games of chance. Seems his little Stella has taken a shine to him."

"You mean Sultry Stell? She's already taken a shine to more blokes than Old Maurice who polishes shoes down on the corner of Kipling Street."

"Terry, please," said Arthur, holding up the half inch stub of his morning cigar in admonishment. "To you she might be Sultry Stell, but to Harry from Barry she's still sweet little Stella in pigtails, home from the gymkhana with her rosettes and ribbons. If he heard you calling her that . . ."

"All right, all right. What's this about her and Kev?"

"It seems your mate Kev has taken a shine to Stella, same as she has to him. She's moved in with him, see, and Harry's worried she might get taken advantage of."

"It's a bit late for him to start worrying about that, innit?" asked Terry.

"I'm talking about financially, Terry," said Arthur impatiently. "Seems when she had it on her toes from the family nest she took some bits of Mrs Evans'. A bracelet, two necklaces, earrings, a pendant. Of great sentimental value, Harry says. About ten grandsworth. He bought them for her as presents in the days when husbands still did things like that for their wives when they'd been caught out at something hooky."

"And Harry wants you to get it back. Knowing Kev, I can see why he's worried."

"That's right. He can't be seen to be interfering himself, though. It might upset Stell."

"All right then, Arthur, I'll go over and have a word."

"It's too late for that, Terry," said Arthur. "Your mate Kev's already got rid of the Evans' family heirlooms. He sold them to me for two grand the day before yesterday."

"Arthur," said Terry in exasperation, "won't you ever learn? Buying gear off Kev. You never thought there might be something iffy about it?"

"He said it was kosher. That he won it off a Greek in a game of brag. Anyway, there's worse to come. I turned the lot over to Soupy Sturridge for a quick monkey."

"Then get on the rag and bone to Soapy and tell him there's been a mistake."

"I already have. He's turned them for another two grand to a pal in the trade. They're in a jeweller's shop window up west with an eight grand price tag on them."

"Then it's down to you, Arthur," said Terry after a moment's silence. "You either buy them back or take a pasting from Harry from Barry and his boys."

"Terry, you're offending my deepest principles with your suggestion," said Arthur. "It seems a steep price to have to pay to save one of your pals from Harry from Barry's wrath."

"You're unbelievable, Arthur," said Terry with contempt. "It's hardly just Kev that you're looking to protect. That isn't why you're down here telling me all this. Anyway, if you explain what happened to this Sturridge geezer maybe he'll chip in a bit. With the monkey you got for selling them yesterday, and the two grand from Kev, you don't stand to come out of it too bad."

"Terry," said Arthur angrily, "you don't seem to understand the . . ."

"Have you got any better ideas?" asked Terry.

They found Soupy Sturridge in his office. His office was the small corner bar of the public house across the road from the house where he rented rooms. Soupy, a short, balding man of seventeen stone who wore a silk waistcoat, was eating his lunch. Across the room, a group of West Indians were involved in a ferocious game of dominoes. Seeing Arthur he beckoned him across to his table. "Forgive me for not rising, Arthur," said Soupy.

"Of course, Soupy, of course, don't let me keep you from your pleasure. Further to our conversation on the telephone this morning . . ."

Arthur talked. Soupy listened.

"I'm sorry, Arthur," he said when Arthur had finished, "but the problem remains your own since I purchased the merchandise from you in good faith. Your argument must surely be the same."

"Look, Soupy, you don't seem to understand," said Terry, grabbing hold of Soupy's arm and halting a dripping wedge of beef on its way towards his mouth. "Little legal niceties like that aren't Harry from Barry's strong point."

Soupy was about to reply when the barman called over and said he was wanted on the phone. "Excuse me a moment, gentlemen," he said with mild impatience, lifting the bottom corner of his serviette to his mouth as he eased his considerable bulk out from behind the table. Terry and

Arthur watched him as, with his napkin still in his collar, he spoke into the telephone in the hallway.

When he returned his urbanity seemed somewhat ruffled and he gazed down at his lunch like Valentino gazing down at a vamp. "It seems fate has intervened, but whether on anyone's behalf or behest is somewhat uncertain," he said after he had regained the rhythm of his eating. "Nevertheless, perhaps we can make a deal. That was Mister Wyman. He has a Mrs Evans in his jeweller's shop who is under the impression that the jewels in the window are her own. Naturally, I have assured him that the good lady is mistaken and she has left now. However, it would be foolish to assume she was convinced, and since, when she returns to claim ownership, I shall be compelled to give my five thousand back to Mr Wyman, I am prepared to compromise."

"Compromise away, Soupy," said Arthur.

"I'll give you one thousand if you go straight to Wyman's and buy the stuff before Mrs Evans gets back."

"Make it fifteen, Soupy," said Arthur.

"You're in no position to bargain, Arthur," observed Soupy. "However, because of the urgency of the situation, I am prepared to raise my offer to twelve."

"Done," said Arthur, then watched Soupy creak forward over his plate, reach a hand into the folds of his voluminous trousers, and bring out two rolls of twenty pound notes which he let fall to his lap. One he gave straight to Arthur, and from the other he pulled ten notes.

"Soupy," said Arthur as he took them, "you're a robber."

"God speed, gentlemen," said Soupy as he returned to his lunch.

Outside, Terry took Arthur's Jag round to Kev's while Arthur took a cab to the jeweller's up west. When Terry got to the end of Kev's street he saw some people kicking up a kerfuffle at Kev's front door, and as he got closer he saw it consisted of Stella putting something in through the letterbox, whilst behind her and with his back to her, Kev was using a dustbin lid to fend off repeated attempts to get past him by two identical men with thick curly hair and creased, grey, matching suits.

Terry stopped the Jag in the middle of the street and got out. He hauled one of the men down onto the pavement and grabbed hold of the other by the shirtcollar. "All right then," said Terry. "If you fancy a bit of it . . ."

"We want our money," said one of the men

"You lost it fair and square, Micky. You and your brother don't know when to stop," said Kev from the top of the stairs.

The two men looked at Terry, then at Kev, then back at Terry. One spoke and they both turned and made their way back down the steps to the street, then across the road to their car, throwing threats and curses back at Kev as they went.

After they had gone, Kev and Stella thanked Terry, and Terry asked who they were. "The Kazantzakis twins," said Kev. "They have to be the most impulsive, hot-headed players in any of the floating games. I knew I could clean up if I could sit down with them. And yesterday I did. You seen Arthur?"

"Yeah, he's looking for you and all," said Terry disapprovingly to Kev.

"I want to buy Stella's jewellery back from him," said Kev.

"Well you're too late for that, my son," said Terry. "Arthur's already got shut."

"The old dog!" said Kev in surprise. "He said he'd hold onto it for a week in case we came back."

"That's why we took the tiny sum he offered for it," said Stella, obviously upset. "I knew Kev would be able to buy it back as soon as he'd played with the Kazantzakis twins. What's Dad going to do now?"

"You don't have to worry about it, Stell," said Terry. "You make some breakfast and I'll explain why."

Later that day, Arthur sat at the bar of *The Winchester* trying to see a bright side to it. Terry let him suffer.

"Twelve from Soupy today. The two grand you managed to get hold of before the Cincinatti Kid could do his worst."

"He told me you were going to hang onto those pieces he sold you for a while to give him a chance to buy them back."

"I did, Terry," said Arthur in a tone of righteous self justification. "But do you think that either you or I could afford to have my working capital tied up and standing idle for a week? I'm surprised he hadn't already frittered it away on the kind of reckless turf investment you favour. Anyway, there's that, and the fee from . . ."

"What fee?" asked Terry.

"Getting back his wife's jewellery put him in one of his 'we'll keep a welcome in the hillside' moods," said Arthur, though it was obvious from his expression that Harry from Barry's generosity had fallen considerably short of making up the balance on the eight grand and the embarrassment he had suffered explaining the situation to Mr Wyman.

"Then if Harry from Barry's paid you, where's my whack?" asked Terry.

"Terence, in the circumstances, is it the act of a fair and honourable man to . . ."

"Oh, fair and honourable, is it?" said Terry. "In that case you won't be asking for any of this then." He took out a brown envelope and put it on the bar. Arthur asked what it was. Terry told him it was the three grand he'd persuaded Kev to give him from his winnings when he'd told him what had happened to Arthur. "Not that you deserve any of it," said Terry. "Now how much was that fee?"

"A hundred," said Arthur and reached for the envelope.

Terry pulled it away.

"Two hundred, Terry, on my word. How much do you want? Fifty? Sixty? Sixty-five?"

"A hundred," said Terry. "And do me a favour, Arthur, next time don't wake me up so early."

Once upon a time in a Minicab

When Terry has done the odd stint as a minicab driver, he often had a laugh at the weird stories told to him by his customers. He didn't believe a lot of them but the teller always insisted they were true. Here are some of the stories he heard. Can you tell which ones are true and which ones are the figments of an overactive imagination?

1. A bizarre case of shoplifting came to light in London one Christmas when a woman fell to the floor at the checkout counter. She was found to have a frozen chicken hidden under her hat.

2. Edward Brookes was sentenced to eighteen months in prison by the Crown Court after pleading guilty to a charge of stealing 35,683 broom handles.

3. Writer Sandra Brown was convicted with a co-defendant for illegally obtaining 10 million dollars with a series of dummy corporations. One of her pieces was entitled *How to Make a Million Before You're Thirty-four.*

4. A man in Davis, California, reported to police that someone had broken into his flat and made a batch of marshmallow treats that were left in the fridge. The burglar also dyed a bowl of rice green.

5. In America, nearly 1,000,000 cars are stolen every year — about one every 30 seconds. Although around half of them are recovered only 14 per cent of the crimes are solved.

6. A burglar in Paris decided, once he'd broken in, to make himself a snack before he got down to business. He washed it down with three bottles of champagne and was arrested the following morning, asleep in the spare room.

7. While working on a building site in Lagos, Nigeria, a labourer decided to alter his pay cheque to get more money. He altered £9–4s–0d to £697,000,090–4s–0d and was arrested.

8. Frustrated at not being able to unlock the door when they attempted a payroll robbery, bandits in Rome fired a machine gun at the lock before fleeing in frustration. Police said the door was unlocked and the bandits had been pulling instead of pushing.

9. Colin Rich pulled three stockings over his head and wrapped his scarf round his face when he went to rob a bank in Ontario. His vision was so restricted that when he reached for his gun he pulled out his spectacle case.

10. A burglar in New Jersey kicked in the door of Mrs Wilma Barnett's home and walked out with a tv set, the kitchen clock, and a fully grown German shepherd watchdog.

Answers: They're all true.

INVASION OF THE 'BODY SCRATCHERS'

"It's what?" asked Arthur, turning the small grey tin round in his hand.

"Ghost In A Can," explained Louie, showing Arthur a crudely drawn wrapper bearing those very words. Underneath, a skeleton in a teddy-boy suit was dancing with what looked like a giant amoeba.

Arthur held the can to his ear and shook it. "There's nothing in here," he said doubtfully. He remembered how Louie's last venture had left him lumbered with two hundred boxes of circular playing cards.

"You've got to unshackle your mind, Arthur," grinned Louie. "The kids will love it. It's my answer to pet rocks and rubber bricks. We print up the labels, drum up a bit of a fuss, and before you know it they'll be trampling over their Cabbage Patch dolls to get one. We could send a couple to the Palace and —"

"I don't want to sound negative," said Arthur, shaking his head, "but I think I'll stick to our original arrangement. Have you got the merchandise?"

Louie opened a large cardboard box and pulled out a small smoked glass bottle. Arthur took it from him, flipped open the lid and sniffed gingerly at the contents. "It's gone off . . ." he complained, holding the bottle at arm's length.

"After shave doesn't go off, Arthur. And the stronger it is, the further it goes."

"I thought you said you'd have the wrappers printed by now."

"They're due tomorrow. And for someone who hasn't even paid a deposit — you're getting a bit choosy, aren't you?"

Arthur reluctantly drew an envelope from his pocket and handed Louie three of the four fifty pound notes inside. Louie held one up to the light.

"Steady on, Louie," said Arthur indignantly. "I've just got those off

Ricky James."

"Tricky Ricky?" asked Louie, inspecting the note more closely. "I didn't know you were interested in second hand shoes, Arthur."

"I'm not," Arthur explained. "Ricky's out of the commodities market. He's running a nightclub now, with his wife. They want Terry to sort out any threshing machine impersonators."

"I always thought Ricky could handle that himself."

"Maybe he's past it," shrugged Arthur. "You know how it is. Some people don't look after themselves. They go to seed. It's all in the mind, you know."

"I know how it is," agreed Louie, watching Arthur stub out his cigar.

Arthur put his feet up on Louie's desk. "Good, then that's settled. Load them up for me while I borrow your phone, will you?"

Terry was at the Palms guest house, unloading the last of a consignment of mattresses when Arthur caught up with him. After a quiet word inside the reception area with the proprietor, Angus Parkinson, Arthur stepped outside where Terry, his eyebrows arched in anticipation, was holding out his hand and rubbing the top of his fingers with his thumb.

"Now I know how this place got its name," muttered Arthur, slapping a bottle of after shave into Terry's hand. "You can have that on account. Worth ten guineas an ounce. Now hurry up and come with me. I'm going to get you a new whistle. I've put you in for an earner that's well tasty."

"Where's my money, Arthur?" asked Terry, as they climbed into Arthur's Jag.

Arthur shook his head vigorously, as if trying to dislodge something from his ear. "Have a sniff of that," he advised, nodding at the bottle in Terry's hand. "One dab of that stuff and you'll have them thinking you're Robert Reynolds."

"£50," Terry persevered. "Just like you promised."

"£30?" asked Arthur exasperatedly, nosing the Jag into traffic. "When did I promise you £50?" He leaned over to Terry with one hand on the wheel. "Go on — try it. It's got a special flip top and — oops!"

"You berk!" said Terry, staring at his soaking trousers as Arthur went back to driving. "This stuff's strong enough to kill a gorilla!" He rolled down his windows as Arthur dabbed at his eyes with a handkerchief.

"You're not meant to splash it all over," he grimaced. "You've got to treat it with respect. Ah, here we are." He pulled up outside a small shop bearing the words TAYLOR'S TAILORING. They walked inside and were met by a tall thin man with a shock of grey hair that would have embarrassed a mad scientist.

"Good to see you, Joseph," said Arthur briskly. "I'd like to hire a suit for my man."

Joseph clasped his hands and beamed. "Arthur, I've got just the thing."

Joseph disappeared into the back room and ten minutes later he and Arthur were sniffing testily as they hovered round the uncomfortable figure of Terry, who was standing in the middle of the shop wearing a dinner suit several sizes too small for him. "I'm not wearing this, Arthur," he said firmly.

"I've got to admit I've seen better fits," agreed Arthur.

"Nonesense, Arthur. This suit could have been made for the boy. This is a suit to enjoy." He tugged lovingly at the back of the jacket and brushed the lapels. Arthur hesitantly joined him, feeling the tightness of the jacket round Terry's chest. His hand stopped when he felt something soft and crinkly through the fabric.

"The last man to hire this suit looked a dream," Joseph continued. "He was an Arabian prince, but in this suit he looked like a king."

"I'm not wearing this suit," Terry insisted.

Arthur held up an authorative finger. "Now don't be too hasty, Terry. If you squeeze yourself up a little and hold your breath that could be a very flattering piece of apparel."

"I'm not wearing it," repeated Terry, his anger rising. A button popped off his jacket, fell to the floor and rolled under a rack of second hand pyjamas.

"Really, Terence," said Arthur, paying Joseph off. "In matters of sartorial taste you'd do well to listen to your elders and betters." He looked impatiently at his watch. "We're too late to start messing about now."

Arthur bustled Terry out of the shop and into the Jag. As Joseph put a CLOSED sign up at his window, Arthur reached over and started putting his hand in Terry's jacket pocket.

"What are you doing?" asked Terry angrily.

Arthur withdrew a roll of old newspaper wrapped with an elastic band. He glowered out of the window as Joseph pulled down the blinds. "That man could crawl up the inside of a drainpipe."

"Never mind all that," said Terry impatiently, scratching under

his shirt. "Either you put some money up front or I'm taking the night off."

"You do for trust what Hitler did for the toothbrush moustache," grumbled Arthur, handing Terry the envelope containing the last fifty pound note. "You know naked greed can be very unappetising—"

"Arthur," urged Terry, pocketing the money, "why don't you stop rabbitting and drive?"

Twenty minutes later, after assuring Tex the Tux — his fellow bouncer — that he hadn't got a tom cat hidden in his pockets, Terry was standing at the door of Ricky James' nightclub and listening half heartedly to a lurid account of the previous evening's events.

"You should have been there when it went off," said Tex enthusiastically. "Never seen anything like it. Wouldn't have missed it for the world."

"Really?" asked Terry, listlessly. He was bored and hot, his suit was too tight, and he was beginning to itch all over.

"Yeah, really. One of them was built like a tank. He picked up a table with one hand and—"

"Hold on," interrupted Terry, staring over Tex's shoulder into the bar. "I think we've got trouble."

Terry was right. A man with a girl on either arm had just been slugged in the belly by a wiry man in a grey suit. As the man tried to kick out in retaliation, he was knocked to the floor by a sharp right hook. The girl started screaming as Terry jumped in. "On your bike, Rocky," said Terry, grabbing the man in the grey suit and pushing him towards Tex. He was turning back to the victim when he noticed one of the girls trying to slip something into her bag. He grabbed her arm and removed the man's wallet from her hand.

"If you don't want the law on your back I'd beat it," he advised, helping the man to his feet. As the two girls fled, Terry felt a gentle tugging on his sleeve.

"That was very good, Terry," said a voice. "I'm Rita James. Would you come into the office?"

"It was nothing," explained Terry as Rita led him up some narrow stairs. "It's an old dodge they use on the tourists."

"Well, you handled yourself very discreetly," smiled Rita, pushing open a door marked PRIVATE. "Sit yourself down while I get you a drink."

Rita disappeared and Terry perched on the arm rest of a deep leather chair. Although the room was small and had no windows, the lighting and the tasteful layout gave off a feeling of space. Terry was admiring a painting of Commanche Run with Lester Piggott on board when he noticed the print was speckled with a dark substance. He held out his hand and touched one of the spots. It was wet. He held up his hand to the light. There was a red smudge on the end of his fingers. He looked at the floor and saw half a red footprint on the rug. A blurred red handmark on the fireplace decided him he was heading for the door when Rita James came back and started screaming like a kettle with a faulty whistle.

In *The Winchester*, Arthur had got sick of waiting for Dave to come back from the cellar and was helping himself to a vodka when Detective Sergeant Chisholm's feet appeared on the stairs. Arthur ducked down behind the bar as Dave came back with a crate of light ale.

"No sign of Public Enemy No. 1?" asked Chisholm, looking round the room. "I don't suppose even Daley's stupid enough to hang around after a stunt like tonight's."

"What are you on about?" asked Dave, placing the crate on the bar.

"Daley. And McCann. They've gone rogue. Cracked Ricky James over the head with an ornamental poker and ran off with the contents of his safe." Chisholm smiled at Dave's incredulous expression. "If you see the bold Arthur, tell him we've got a nice cold cell waiting for him, right next to his mate's. Rita James is squawking like a mother hen on a Rubik cube."

Arthur came up white faced and shivering when Chisholm disappeared. He didn't even seem to hear Dosshouse Donlan's elaborate apology for the reconstituted mattresses he'd sold him. He gulped down his vodka and, ignoring Dave's well-meaning advice, staggered to the phone. After three breathless, desperate calls he'd found out which hospital Ricky James was in.

At the hospital, Arthur took a white coat from a cupboard and, after skulking in closets and ducking down empty passageways for two hours, finally located Ricky in a room at the end of a crowded ward. He slid through the partially open door and made his way to Ricky's bedside. Ricky lay motionless, his head swathed in bandages. In the faint glow from the corridor, Arthur saw that his eyes were open, glittering in the half light like two shiny, hard-backed beetles on a bowl of tripe. "Ricky?" he whispered. No answer. Arthur crouched by the bed and explained everything that had happened.

"What!" blurted Ricky, his face darkening. He was wheezing like a rusty bicycle pump. "It's Rita!" he continued, struggling to get up.

Arthur pushed him back on the bed and put his finger to his lips. "She's set you and Terry up," Ricky growled angrily. "And all because of that fur coat. She knows I don't like cruelty to animals."

"Very commendable, Ricky. But what can we do? She's already made a statement implicating Terry." Arthur's eyes kept scanning the doorway for any movement.

Ricky's breath came thick, noisy and fast. "There's just one thing. She doesn't know I know about it. It happened so long ago she thinks she's in the clear. If she knew that you knew she'd drop the charges." He gulped for air and a dry rattling sounded in his throat.

"Well," urged Arthur impatiently, "what is it?"

Ricky's tongue came out and he grasped his throat with one hand as the other held Arthur's forearm in a vice-like grip. His breathing got louder and more irregular. "It's . . . it's . . ." His shivering, nodding head strained upwards.

"Yes, yes?" encouraged Arthur.

Ricky seemed to go purple with the effort of lifting his head off the pillow. He let go of Arthur's arm and reached out ahead of him, as if stretching to touch some far off light. His eyes began to roll. "It's . . . it's . . . it's . . . it's . . ." Suddenly there was a strangled croak from Ricky's mouth and his head fell backwards on its side.

Arthur felt like his innards had been grabbed by a gigantic icy fist. "Ricky!" he hissed, putting his ear to Ricky's heart. He couldn't hear a beat. His own heart seemed to be having palpitations as he peered in horror into Ricky's apparently sightless eyes. "Ricky! Wake up!" Arthur slapped Ricky's slack jaw. "Wake up! You can't do this to me. You can't—" Arthur's protestations turned into a howl of shock and fear as the lights in the ward suddenly flooded on. He stepped back from the bed as if it were wired to the mains.

"What are you doing?" demanded the nurse, striding purposefully to the bed.

"I . . . er . . . he . . . he seemed to be choking," Arthur explained, taking a wide course towards the door. The nurse was vigorously manipulating Ricky's chest as Arthur began slipping off the white coat. There was a noise like a wellington boot freeing itself from thick mud, another more alarming one that carried traces of both bull moose and bagpipes, and as Arthur dived through the door and raced down the corridor, Ricky's voice could be heard booming over the entire ward. "Brighton, Arthur! Brighton '66!"

Arthur was still trying to make sense of it when he rushed round the corner and bumped into Detective Sergeant Chisholm. Arthur

stood clutching his heart and gasping, slurping white-faced for breath as a slow smile formed on Chisholm's face and he reached out and felt Arthur's collar. "Gotcha!"

Down at the police station, with Arthur and Terry on chairs by the wall and Sergeant Chisholm facing Rita across his desk, the policeman's anger was being cranked up yet another notch by the nightclub hostess' less than coherent testimony.

"This story is getting more holes in it than a fakir's hot water bottle," he complained testily. "You've already said you caught McCann in the act, and everyone knows that wherever McCann is, this piece of verminous slime is creeping round the shadows. Look at his face. If his lips are moving you know he's lying."

"I'm just not sure any more," sobbed Rita into a big red handkerchief. "I'm so confused. It's the shock. The shock. Poor, poor Ricky." She held the handkerchief to her face and shot Arthur a quick look over the top. Arthur smiled and pushed his hat back on his head. Terry stared stonily at the floor with his arms folded.

"There, there," said Arthur comfortingly. "I know things must be a terrible muddle. But Ricky's going to be all right now. Are you sure you can't remember anything about giving me that money to hire Terry?"

Rita glared evilly at him and wailed into her hanky. She blew her nose and a distant tugboat echoed the sound. "It's such a tangle in my mind . . I can't seem to think. The only thing I can truly remember is that smell . . . that awful, horrid smell . . ."

Chisholm sighed and picked up a pencil from his desk. "Getting sense from you is like drying yourself with a plastic bag."

"The Sergeant's right," said Arthur kindly. "You should concentrate. Like Ricky. He said the only thing that kept him going was the thought of Brighton . . . Brighton '66."

The colour drained from Rita's face and she swallowed noisily. She shook her head, a light seemed to grow in her eyes and she studied her surroundings as if coming out of a dream. "Wh-where am I?" she asked, pausing with her fingertips to her cheeks. "Of course! Oh no! I remember now! I did give you the money to give to Terry! It must have been . . ."

"The shock?" nodded Arthur, as Chisholm's pencil snapped angrily on the other side of the desk.

Three hours later, as the early morning sun took the chill of the night off the slowly wakening streets, and Rita James stayed behind to answer further questions, Arthur and Terry were walking past the Palms guest house towards a celebration breakfast when Angus Parkinson came running angrily down the steps. "Those mattresses you sold me, Arthur," he said indignantly. "They were alive!"

Arthur held up his hands. "I know," he said gravely. "It's unforgivable. Heads will roll. My investigators tell me infestation occurred in transit from the Swedish manufacturers, and already my lawyers are talking to the airline concerned. Rest assured that the company will pay handsomely to avoid implicating its most famous and prestigious name with such a squalid episode. And until full restitution can be made —" Arthur pulled a bottle of after shave from his pocket, "the finest pesticide known to science can be yours on the most reasonable of terms."

"So it was the mattresses," said Terry, when they were out of earshot. "I thought it was the suit."

"No," smiled Arthur, careful to keep his distance. "Joseph's suit didn't give you fleas — you gave the fleas to that thieving ratbag's suit. Pop it in a plastic bag and take it back to him."

"I wouldn't like to see his face when he finds out," said Terry doubtfully.

"He won't find out from me, Terence. But I do admit I wouldn't mind seeing the crooked toerag's ugly mug when his next customer brings it back."

Terry watched as Arthur walked down the street with a beatific smile on his face. It stayed there in place, seamless and invincible, right up to the moment he felt the first uncontrollable urge to scratch at the sudden itching sensation on his knee.

JOE 'N' ANNE, THE BARBARIANS

When the fight at the wedding party got out of control, Joe London and his bride of fifteen minutes, Anne, suddenly forgot their differences and took the nearest person — Arthur, on his way home after selling 4 gross of hamster-sized flea collars — hostage in a derelict house. The people at the party were out